I0819411

Living the Little Way

Living the Little Way

Six Keys to the Spirituality of St. Thérèse

Fr. Joseph Spence, FFm

TAN Books
Gastonia, North Carolina

Cover design by Jordan Avery

ISBN: 978-1-5051-3724-8
ePUB ISBN: 978-1-5051-3974-7

Published in the United States by
TAN Books
PO Box 269
Gastonia, NC 28053

www.TANBooks.com

Printed in India

"The whole world will love me."

—SAINT THÉRÈSE OF LISIEUX

CONTENTS

ABBREVIATIONS

Writings and Sources of St. Thérèse of Lisieux

CJ ***Carnet Jaune*** (*Yellow Notebook*) of Mother Agnes of Jesus, in: SAINT THÉRÈSE OF LISIEUX, *Her Last Conversations*, Translated by JOHN CLARKE, OCD, ICS Publications, Washington, D.C. 1977.

CSG ***Conseils et Souvenirs*** *(Advice and Memoirs)* of Sister Geneviève, in: *My Sister St. Thérèse, by Sister Geneviève of the Holy Face (Celine Martin)*, Authorized Translation by the Carmelite Sisters of New York of *Conseils et Souvenirs*, Tan Books and Publishers, Inc., Rockford, Illinois 1997.

LT ***Letters*** from Thérèse, in: SAINT THÉRÈSE OF LISIEUX, *General Correspondence.*

Volume I (1877-1890), Translated by JOHN CLARKE, OCD, ICS Publications, Washington, D.C. 1982; SAINT THÉRÈSE OF LISIEUX, *General Correspondence. Volume II (1890-1897)*, Translated by JOHN CLARKE, OCD, ICS Publications, Washington, D.C. 1988.

Ms A ***Manuscript* A**: Autobiographical Manuscript dedicated to Mother Agnes of Jesus, in: *Story of a Soul. The Autobiography of Saint Thérèse of Lisieux* (Translated from the original manuscripts by JOHN CLARKE, OCD). A Study Edition prepared by MARC FOLEY, OCD, ICS Publications, Washington, D.C. 2019.

Ms B ***Manuscript* B**: Letter to Sister Marie of the Sacred Heart, in: *Story of a Soul. The Autobiography of Saint Thérèse of Lisieux* (Translated from the original manuscripts by JOHN CLARKE, OCD). A Study Edition prepared by MARC FOLEY, OCD, ICS Publications, Washington, D.C. 2019.

Ms C ***Manuscript* C**: Autobiographical Manuscript dedicated to Mother Marie de Gonzague, in: *Story of a Soul. The Autobiography of Saint*

Thérèse of Lisieux (Translated from the original manuscripts by JOHN CLARKE, OCD). A Study Edition prepared by MARC FOLEY, OCD, ICS Publications, Washington, D.C. 2019.

P **Poems** of St. Thérèse of the Child Jesus, in: *The Poetry of Saint Thérèse of Lisieux. Complete Edition. Texts and Introductions,* Translated by Donald Kinney, OCD, ICS Publications, Washington, D.C. 1996.

Pr **Prayers** of Saint Thérèse of the Child Jesus, in: *The Prayers of Saint Thérèse of Lisieux,* General Introduction by GUY GAUCHER, OCD, Translated by Aletheia Kane, OCD, ICS Publications, Washington, D.C. 1997.

PR **Pious Recreations** of St. Thérèse of the Child Jesus, in: *The Plays of Saint Thérèse of Lisieux. "Pious Recreations",* General Introduction by GUY GAUCHER, OCD, Translated by SUSAN CONROY AND DAVID J. DWYER, ICS Publications, Washington, D.C. 2008.

INTRODUCTION

What more can be said of St. Thérèse of the Child Jesus and of the Holy Face? Why another book on Thérèse? Why *this* book on Thérèse? These valid questions demand an answer.

I believe that the answer is threefold. One aspect regards Thérèse and her doctrine. A second consideration takes into account the world as it is today. The third reason is based on studies already done (or not done) on Thérèse.

On October 19, 1997, Pope St. John Paul II officially declared Thérèse as the youngest Doctor of the Church.[1] Her "science of love," her doctrine, is thus universally valid and important. The Doctors of the

---

1 See: The Apostolic Letter of His Holiness Pope John Paul II, *Divini Amoris Scientia*. Cf. https://www.vatican.va/content/john-paul-ii/en/apost_letters/1997/documents/hf_jp-ii_apl_19101997_divini-amoris.html (Consulted on March 27th 2025).

> way and my soul was like a book in which this priest read better than I did myself. He launched me full sail upon the waves of *confidence and love* which so strongly attracted me, but upon which I dared not advance.[21]

Thérèse could now "sail" freely upon the waves of "confidence and love"! But her soul was not quite ready yet. It was still growing and maturing in the crucible of many sufferings, especially the sickness of her dear father, Louis. In the meantime, the Prioress Mother Marie de Gonzague's strange and tyrannous way of governing the Carmel did not encourage such sentiments of confidence and love. Thérèse confided in her *Manuscript* A, addressed to her sister Pauline, just a few lines after recounting her confession with Fr. Alexis Prou: "My nature was such that fear made me recoil; with *love* not only did I advance, I actually *flew*. O Mother, it was especially since the blessed day

---

[21] Saint Thérèse of Lisieux, *Autobiographical Manuscript dedicated to Mother Agnes of Jesus*, in *Story of a Soul: The Autobiography of Saint Thérèse of Lisieux*, trans. John Clarke, OCD, A Study Edition prepared by Marc Foley, OCD (Washington, D.C.: ICS Publications, 2019), 80.

Church—more so than other saints—have an experience and a doctrine that is something like a goldmine. Thankfully, the search for their wisdom is no exploitation; rather, it's a noble pursuit: "Choose my instruction instead of silver, knowledge rather than choice gold, for wisdom is more precious than rubies, and nothing you desire can compare with her" (Prov. 8:10-11). A goldmine is destined to terminate its yield, whereas, in the case of the Doctors of the Church, and thus of Thérèse, their wealth is practically interminable. It's a question of knowing how to extract it well.

The second response to the questions above lies in the contemporary world and its needs. In 2023, Pope Francis promulgated an entire Apostolic Exhortation dedicated solely to Thérèse and to her teachings: *C'est la confiance.*[2] At the end of the document, Pope Francis invited all believers to draw from Thérèse's doctrine and insight:

---

2 Pope Francis, *C'est la confiance: Apostolic Exhortation on Confidence in the Merciful Love of God for the 150th Anniversary of the Birth of St. Thérèse of the Child Jesus and the Holy Face*, October 15, 2023, accessed March 27, 2025, https://www.vatican.va/content/francesco/en/apost_exhortations/documents/20231015-santateresa-delbambinogesu.html

> As theologians, moralists and spiritual writers, as pastors and as believers, wherever we find ourselves, we need constantly to appropriate this insight of Thérèse and to draw from it consequences both theoretical and practical, doctrinal and pastoral, personal and communal. We need boldness and interior freedom to do so.[3]

The world is needful, according to Pope Francis, of Thérèse's insight and wisdom. I certainly agree!

C'est la confiance, Pope Francis's Apostolic Exhortation on Thérèse, was promulgated on the 150th anniversary of her birth (January 2, 1873–October 15, 2023). On the same occasion, the *United Nations Educational, Scientific, and Cultural Organization* (UNESCO) recognized Thérèse, particularly in the years 2022–2023, as a World Heritage Person. Moreover, 2025 was the centenary of Thérèse's Canonization, solemnly celebrated by Pope Pius XI on May 17, 1925. The Catholic Church and world-renowned organizations, such as the UNESCO, thus recognize in Thérèse a leading figure for today's cultural and spiritual welfare.

---

3 Francis, *C'est la confiance*, no. 50.

Let us now come to the third and final reason behind the publication of this study on Thérèse. It regards the studies done—or not done—on Thérèse so far. Yet, we must take a brief step back to have a view of the entire "picture" as it were. The topics chosen for this book try to offer a sort of "key," or rather six "keys," to more easily penetrate the sanctuary of Thérèse's heart and soul. They had to capture, therefore, at least some of the main elements of her spirituality. Still, only two of the topics have already been widely researched and discussed: namely, her "Little Way" and her devotion to the Child Jesus.

The other topics, that is, her devotion to the Holy Face; the theme "Jesus as Spouse and Thérèse"; the relationship between Thérèse and the Blessed Virgin Mary; her "fraternal charity"; and her "Passion" and death, have actually *not* been widely or deeply researched as of yet. This could seem surprising, yet so it is. Leaving aside a few articles which broach these subjects—articles are always purposefully incomplete—we must quote a few books to briefly demonstrate this point.

One book—that is, one doctoral thesis—has been published regarding Thérèse and the Holy Face.[4]

---

4 Cyprien Niyitegeka, *The Metaphor of the Face in Thérèse of Lisieux from the Philosophical Perspective of Emmanuel*

However, it does not seem to delve deeply into Thérèse's own experience, but only in a peripheral way and from a philosophical point of view. I do not know of any book directly regarding, instead, the theme of "Jesus as Spouse" and Thérèse.[5] The same must be said regarding Thérèse and the Blessed Virgin Mary.[6]

Instead, one good book has been published regarding Thérèse's "fraternal charity": the Theresian expert Fr. Pierre Descouvemont's *Thérèse de Lisieux et son prochain*[7] (*Thérèse of Lisieux and her neighbor*). However, it is only available in French. And, as far as Thérèse's "Passion" is concerned, thankfully, one great book

---

Lévinas: Creating a Model for Contemporary Mission Spirituality (PhD diss., The Catholic University of America, 2017).

5 Joseph Spence, *Un'esperienza sponsale con Dio: l'influsso di san Giovanni della Croce su santa Teresa di Lisieux* (doctoral diss., Teresianum, Rome, 2019–20). English title: *A Spousal Experience with God: The Influence of St. John of the Cross on St. Thérèse of Lisieux*. See also C. Ermatinger, *St. Thérèse of Lisieux, Spouse and Victim* (Washington, DC: ICS Publications, 2010).

6 M. E. Patrizi, *Il Patto segreto: L'amicizia mistica di san Massimiliano Kolbe e santa Teresa di Lisieux* (Rome: C.d.C. Editrice, 2008).

7 P. Descouvemont, *Thérèse de Lisieux et son prochain* (Paris: Les Éditions du Cerf, 2003).

has been published, by the world-renowned expert on Thérèse, Bishop Guy Gaucher, OCD, *The Passion of Thérèse of Lisieux*.[8]

This glance at the world of studies on Thérèse helps one to understand the need to still deepen—surprisingly enough—various important topics regarding this young and inspiring Doctor of the Church. Therefore, without further ado, we must now delve into Thérèse's own experience and words. My aim is to let Thérèse speak for herself: the facts regarding her life, her *Writings*, and the testimonies of those who knew her will be the main and wholesome ingredients for this new spiritual "dessert," hopefully both short and sweet, yet equally nourishing!

---

8 Guy Gaucher, *The Passion of Thérèse of Lisieux* (New York: The Crossroad Publishing Company, 1990).

From left to right: Céline and Thérèse Martin (1881). Thérèse was 8 years old in this picture.[9] © Archives du Carmel de Lisieux. Used with permission.

---

9 Carmel of Lisieux Archives, "Photographs of St. Thérèse of the Child Jesus and of the Holy Face," accessed March 27, 2025, https://archives.carmeldelisieux.fr/en/.

CHAPTER ONE

St. Thérèse's "Little Way"

1. Introduction: confidence in God's mercy in a "hostile" spiritual climate

"The whole world will love me," Thérèse said to her sister Pauline two months before her death.[10] Enthusiasm? Fantasy? No—prophecy. It is Thérèse's "Little Way," her understanding of "God's gentleness," I think, that captivates everyone who chances upon her—believers and non-believers—and, oftentimes, changes their way of perceiving God. If God is good and gentle, tender and merciful, then one can trust Him; or rather, entrust oneself to Him with total confidence and abandonment, like a child in his mother's

[10] St. Thérèse of Lisieux, *Her Last Conversations*, trans. John Clarke, O.C.D. (Washington, DC: ICS Publications, 1977), 126.

(or father's) arms. How was it, then, that in a time in France when Jansenism was rampant, Thérèse could have understood and experienced God from a totally different point of view? Jansenism was the current trend of pseudo-spirituality that portrayed God as a distant and punishing Judge, not to be approached too closely or with too much confidence. The spiritual atmosphere, even in the Carmel of Lisieux where Thérèse lived, was imbued with Jansenism. Let's take a closer look at Thérèse's experience to better understand the genesis and the meaning of her "Little Way," prophetic both for her time and for today.

2. The "roots" of Thérèse's "Little Way": the Martin family

If it is true that our mother and our father help us to understand who God is, then certainly Thérèse had an advantage in that sense: she would later write that "God gave me a father and a mother more worthy of heaven than of earth."[11] Unfortunately, the sweet exchange of love and affection between Thérèse and her dear mother, so important for Thérèse's growth in

---

[11] Saint Thérèse of Lisieux, *General Correspondence*, vol. 1 (1877–1890), trans. John Clarke, OCD (Washington, D.C.: ICS Publications, 1982), 261.

the time of her infancy, soon came to an abrupt and premature end. Her mother, Zélie, had advanced and incurable breast cancer. Yet during her time on earth, their relationship was one full of love and affection, as seen in Zélie's letter to Pauline, the second-born of the family:

> The other day I wanted to kiss Thérèse before going downstairs. She seemed to be in a deep sleep, and I didn't dare wake her up when Marie said to me, "Mama, she's pretending to be asleep, I'm sure of it." Then, I bent down over her forehead to kiss her, but she immediately hid herself under the blanket, saying to me, sounding like a spoiled child, "I don't want anyone to look at me." I was less than pleased, and I let her know it. Two minutes later I heard her crying, and the next thing I knew, to my great surprise, I saw her at my side! She'd left her little bed all by herself and came down the stairs barefoot, encumbered by her nightgown which was longer than she was. Her little face was covered in tears. "Mama," she said, while throwing herself at my knees, "I was naughty,

> forgive me!" Forgiveness was quickly given. I took my little angel in my arms, pressing her to my heart and covering her with kisses. When she saw herself so well received, she said to me, "Oh! Mama, if only you wanted to wrap me in a blanket like when I was little! I'd eat my chocolate here at the table." I took the trouble to go look for her blanket and then I wrapped her in it like when she was little. I looked like I was playing with a doll![12]

Six months later, Zélie died when Thérèse was only four years old. Her father had to compensate, as Thérèse later wrote in her Manuscript A: "[After our mother's death], our father's *very affectionate* heart seemed to be enriched now with a truly maternal love!".

Thérèse was, in the end, the last-born of the family: the "Benjamin" as she was often nicknamed. To be truthful, her elder sisters—especially Marie and Pauline—treated her as the baby of the family until her death. And, in some way, Thérèse identified herself

---

12 Carmel of Lisieux Archives, "Letter of Zélie Guérin Martin to Pauline, February 13, 1877," accessed March 27, 2025, https://archives.carmeldelisieux.fr/en/correspondance/de-mme-martin-a-pauline-cf-188-13-fevrier-1877/

in this role and position that she naturally held in the family. However, it would be far too reductive or simplistic to say that Thérèse's "Little Way" was inspired simply by the fact that she was the "baby" of the family.

3. Early signs and developments of the "Little Way"

Where then—besides in her family life—can we find the first traces or signs of what would later become Thérèse's "Little Way"? A glance at her *Letters*, even during the time of her adolescence, already reveals some explicit "traces" of elements that would later develop and form her "Little Way." During her pilgrimage to Rome—in the hopes of receiving the pope's permission to enter Carmel at only 15 years of age—Thérèse started referring to herself as the "little ball" and the "little toy" of the Child Jesus. "I am the Child Jesus' little ball; if he wishes to break His toy, He is free. Yes, I will all that He wills,"[13] she wrote to Pauline. During the same pilgrimage to Rome, other signs or key words can be found flowing from Thérèse's pen in that time of trial: in a particular way, the term

---

[13] St. Thérèse of Lisieux, *General Correspondence*, vol. 1: *1887–1890*, Letter 36, 353.

confiance ("confidence"). She wrote to her Aunt Madame Guérin:

> I don't know how I'll go about speaking to the Pope [. . .]. Really, if God were not to take charge of all, I don't know how I would do it. But I have such a great confidence in Him that He will not be able to abandon me; I'm placing all in His hands.[14]

Upon her return to Lisieux, after her unsuccessful trip to Rome, Thérèse wrote to Bishop Hugonin, requesting, once again, entrance into Carmel. "Oh, Mon-seigneur! Christmas is approaching, but I am awaiting your answer with great confidence (*confiance*)."[15] Littleness; abandonment to God's will; confidence, trust, and hope in God: are not these the fundamental elements of Thérèse's "Little Way"? Shortly before her entrance into Carmel, Thérèse starts substituting the image of the "little toy" or "little ball" of Jesus with that of the "little grain of sand."

---

[14] St. Thérèse of Lisieux, *General Correspondence*, vol. 1: *1887–1890*, Letter 32 (November 14, 1887).

[15] St. Thérèse of Lisieux, *General Correspondence*, vol. 1: *1887–1890*, Letter 38B (December 3–8, 1887).

On March 27, 1888, she wrote to her sister, Sr. Agnes of Jesus: "Oh! yes, Pauline, I always want to be the LITTLE grain of sand."[16]

4. Further developments of the "Little Way" in Carmel

And so Thérèse's "Little Way" slowly started to take form and grow. In the first few years of Thérèse's religious life in Carmel, her "Little Way" was still, as it were, in hibernation, or rather, in "incubation." From her entrance in Carmel in April of 1888 (at 15 years of age), until the year 1893 (at 20 years of age), we can only catch a few glimpses of her "Little Way," in that gradual process of growth and maturation typical of

---

16 St. Thérèse of Lisieux, *General Correspondence*, vol. 1: *1887–1890*, Letter 45 (March 27, 1888). It's interesting to keep in mind that both images—that of the "little ball" of Jesus, and that of the "little grain of sand"—were not invented by Thérèse: they were quoted in two different prayers that she came to know and love. (The same must be said for the name she gave herself: the "Little Flower." She was inspired by a holy card with a prayer, *The Little Flower of the Divine Prisoner*, given to her by her sister Céline on the day of her First Communion.) For the prayers referenced, see St. Thérèse of Lisieux, *General Correspondence*, vol. 2: *1890–1897*, trans. John Clarke, O.C.D. (Washington, DC: ICS Publications, 2014), 1277–81.

the ways of nature and of the ways of the Holy Spirit (in the lives of men). In July of 1888, Thérèse wrote to Pauline (Sr. Agnes of Jesus), speaking of herself in the third person: "Its weakness gives rise to all its confidence (*confiance*)."[17] In May of 1889, almost a year later, she wrote to her cousin Marie Guérin: "What offends [Jesus] and what wounds His Heart is the lack of *confiance*!".[18] On the day of her Profession, September 8, 1890, Thérèse wrote in her *Profession Note*: "Let me be looked on as one to be trampled underfoot, forgotten like your little grain of sand, Jesus" (Pr 2). The day before, in a letter to her sister Marie (Sr. Marie of the Sacred Heart), Thérèse had defined herself as the "little spouse" of Jesus.[19]

Several months passed before we see another glimpse of the "Little Way" in Thérèse: in April of 1891, now 18 years old, Thérèse wrote to her sister Céline, quoting the Gospel of Matthew 11:25: "Together we grew up; together Jesus instructed us

---

[17] St. Thérèse of Lisieux, *General Correspondence*, vol. 1: *1887–1890*, Letter 55 (July 5–9, 1888).

[18] St. Thérèse of Lisieux, *General Correspondence*, vol. 1: *1887–1890*, Letter 92 (May 30, 1889).

[19] St. Thérèse of Lisieux, *General Correspondence*, vol. 1: *1887–1890*, Letter 116 (September 7, 1890).

in His secrets, sublime secrets that He hides from the mighty and reveals to the little ones (*aux petits*)."[20]

5. A providential encounter with Fr. Alexis Prou

The first five years of Thérèse's religious life pass by with only a few hints to her "Little Way." This is due to a precise reason: it was growing, slowly but surely, in the depths of her heart, but not without a struggle. The climate of spiritual fear caused by Jansenism was strong, even in the Carmel of Lisieux. How could Thérèse be freed from these spiritual fetters surrounding her? In October of the same year, Thérèse had an encounter which was to become fundamental for her spiritual journey: her two confessions with Fr. Alexis Prou, the Franciscan preacher of the Spiritual Exercises that year. Thérèse would later write in her *Manuscript* A:

> I felt disposed to say nothing of my interior dispositions since I didn't know how to express them, but I had hardly entered the confessional when I felt my soul expand. After speaking only a few words, *I was understood* in a marvelous

[20] St. Thérèse of Lisieux, *General Correspondence*, vol. 1: *1887–1890*, Letter 127 (April 26, 1891).

of your election [as Prioress] that I have flown in the ways of love."[22]

Fr. Alexis Prou.

6. A new spiritual "springtime"

At the beginning of February 1893, at 20 years of age, her "Little Way" started to bud, as if in an anticipated springtime. Upon insistent request of a fellow nun in the Lisieux Carmel, Sr. Theresa of Saint-Augustin, Thérèse wrote her first poem, "The Divine Dew, or The Virginal Milk of Mary":

---

[22] Thérèse of Lisieux, *Autobiographical Manuscript dedicated to Mother Agnes of Jesus,* 80.

My Sweet Jesus, You appear to me
On your Mother's breast, all radiant with love.
Love is the ineffable mystery
That exiled you from your Heavenly Home . . .
Ah! let me hide myself under the veil
Concealing you from all mortal eyes,
And near you, O Morning Star!
I shall find a foretaste of Heaven.[23]

In her chaste yet audacious language, Thérèse desired to become a child, so as to nurse from Mary's breasts together with Jesus. How not to think of the Song of Songs, Chapter 8: "If only you were to me like a brother, who was nursed at my mother's breasts! Then, if I found you outside, I would kiss you, and no one would despise me." (We'll look deeper at Thérèse's chaste and passionate love for Jesus as her "Spouse" in Chapter 3.)

In the years 1893 and 1894, Thérèse's "Little Way" slowly but surely "sprouts" and grows in her heart and mind. Her *Letters* in this time period testify to this. In July of 1893, she wrote to Céline:

---

[23] *The Poetry of Saint Thérèse of Lisieux. Complete Edition. Texts and Introductions*, Translated by Donald Kinney, OCD, ICS Publications, Washington, D.C. 1996.

> Directors have others advance in perfection by having them perform a great number of acts of virtue, and they are right; but my director, who is Jesus, teaches me not to count up my acts. He teaches me to do *all* through love, to refuse Him nothing, to be content when He gives me a chance of proving to Him that I love Him. But this is done in peace, in *abandonment*, it is Jesus who is doing all in me, and I do nothing.[24]

Thérèse's spiritual director, then, was Jesus Himself. Jesus *Himself* directed her soul. It was He, in the end, who taught Thérèse her "Little Way."

7. 1894: a pivotal year

The year 1894 proved to be a pivotal and milestone year in the formation of Thérèse's "Little Way." Céline Martin, Thérèse's sister, "soul-mate," and pen-pal, finally entered the Carmel of Lisieux on September 14, 1894. And what did she bring with her? Besides her camera, innovative and, I would say, providential machinery for seeing Thérèse as she really was, Céline brought

---

[24] St. Thérèse of Lisieux, *General Correspondence*, vol. 1: *1887–1890*, Letter 142 (July 6, 1893).

something else equally important: a small notebook bound in black leather,[25] which was later called *Céline's Notebook*. Céline had copied down various passages of the Old Testament from one of the two Bibles that the Martin family disposed of. In the Lisieux Carmel, it was difficult to get one's hands on the Bible, especially the Old Testament. With *Céline's Notebook*, Thérèse could enjoy selected passages of the Old Testament without having to ask permission from anyone! Two passages of this notebook made a great—even a life-changing (in a good sense)—impression upon Thérèse, serving as a confirmation and a catalyst for her "Little Way": Proverbs 9:4 and Isaiah 66:12–13.

Conrad De Meester stresses the importance of this "discovery" in his book, *The Power of Confidence*.[26] Thérèse effectively found in these two passages of Sacred Scripture the answer, the response that she was looking for. She would later write in her *Manuscript* C:

---

[25] Guy Gaucher, introduction to *La Bible avec Thérèse de Lisieux*, ed. Sœur Cécile du Carmel de Lisieux and Sœur Geneviève, O.P., du monastère de Clairefontaine (Paris: Les Éditions du Cerf, 1990), 9–41, at 20 (where he speaks of Céline's notebook).

[26] Conrad De Meester, *The Power of Confidence: Genesis and Structure of the "Way of Spiritual Childhood" of Saint Thérèse of Lisieux*, trans. Susan Conroy (New York: Alba House, 1998).

We are now living in the age of inventions, and we no longer have to take the trouble of climbing stairs, for, in the homes of the rich, an elevator has replaced these very successfully. I wanted to find an elevator which would raise me to Jesus, for I am too small to climb the rough stairway of perfection. I searched, then, in the scriptures for some sign of this elevator, the object of my desires, and I read these words coming from the mouth of Eternal Wisdom: "*Whoever is a LITTLE ONE, let him come to me.*" And so I succeeded. I felt I had found what I was looking for. But wanting to know, O my God, what You would do to *the very little one* who answered Your call, I continued my search and this is what I discovered: "*As one whom a mother caresses, so will I comfort you; you shall be carried at the breasts, and upon the knees they shall caress you.*" Ah! never did words more tender and more melodious come to give joy to my soul. The elevator which must raise me to heaven is Your arms, O Jesus! And for this I had no need to grow

> up, but rather I had to remain *little* and become this more and more.[27]

"I had to remain *little* and become this more and more." De Meester argues that Thérèse made this discovery shortly after Céline's entrance, and certainly by the end of the year 1894. In the following period, in fact, Thérèse uses the expression "very little" five times in her *Letters* to define herself and her ideal.[28]

8. Sources and Influences in the formation of Thérèse's "Little Way"

So, all things considered, what were the various sources and influences that helped Thérèse to form her "Little Way"? In reality, they were many: certainly her family and her holy parents; the spirituality of the time, along with the three prayers that struck Thérèse since her childhood and even into the first years of Carmel, as mentioned earlier; most probably certain passages of the *Imitation of Christ* (which Thérèse knew almost by

---

[27] Autobiographical Manuscript dedicated to Mother Marie de Gonzague, in *Story of a Soul: The Autobiography of Saint Thérèse of Lisieux*, trans. John Clarke, OCD, study ed. Marc Foley, OCD (Washington, D.C.: ICS Publications, 2019), 2v°–3v°.

[28] De Meester, *The Power of Confidence*, 31–35.

heart) regarding humility and love for Christ; St. John of the Cross and his many teachings on humility and true love for God, which Thérèse avidly and deeply drew from; and the same mysteries of Christ that formed Thérèse's religious name (the Child Jesus and the Holy Face) were highly influential: they describe and remind us of the *kenosis* (self-emptying) of Christ and His hiddenness in this world. To some extent, the mystery of the "Child Jesus" represents the epitome of Thérèse's "Little Way."[29] And the episode of Jesus who calls upon and blesses the children, present in all three of the Synoptic Gospels,[30] was particularly dear

---

29 Céline Martin (Sr. Geneviève of the Holy Face), *My Sister St. Thérèse*, authorized trans. Carmelite Sisters of New York of *Conseils et Souvenirs* (Rockford, IL: Tan Books and Publishers, 1997), 46–47. Céline recalls: "The name Thérèse de l'Enfant Jésus which had been promised to her at the age of nine when she expressed a desire to become a Carmelite during her visit with the Prioress, Mère Marie de Gonzague, had a definite meaning for her and she constantly endeavored to become worthy of it." A few lines earlier, she also wrote: "But it was the Mystery of the Infant Jesus in the Crib at Bethlehem that was her special delight, for it was there that He was in the habit of whispering to her all His secrets about simplicity and abandonment."

30 Cf. Matt. 19:13–15; Mark 10:13–16; Luke 18:15–17.

to Thérèse. As a matter of fact, it is most importantly the Holy Scriptures that inspired Thérèse in her "Little Way." Since 1892—that is, since Thérèse turned nineteen years of age—she preferred the Gospels as her main source of spiritual nourishment.[31] It was the Holy Spirit Himself, then, and Jesus, Thérèse's "spiritual director," who instructed Thérèse in the depths of her heart, soul, and mind—through the Holy Scriptures, first and foremost, and through various other sources—forging in her a beautifully correct image of God. Something radical (in a good sense) and surprising, different and prophetic in a time and place poisoned by Jansenism—that is, by a false image of God.

9. The "Little Way"

Now, what exactly does this "Little Way" consist of? Or rather, what drove Thérèse to search for it, to develop it, to teach it to her novices and spiritual brothers, and to prophesy that her "Little Way" would have been useful for many "little souls" in the future? I would say that Thérèse's "Little Way" all starts with

---

[31] See the *Chronologie* (Timeline) of Thérèse in: *Sainte Thérèse de l'Enfant-Jésus et de la Sainte-Face: Œuvres complètes (Textes et Dernières Paroles)* (Lonrai: Éditions du Cerf/Desclée De Brouwer, 1992), 1491.

an inspiration, a desire that God Himself placed in Thérèse's heart. She wrote, in her *Manuscript* A:

> When reading the accounts of the patriotic deeds of the French heroines, especially the *Venerable* JOAN OF ARC, I had a great desire to imitate them; and it seemed I felt within me the same burning zeal with which they were animated, the same heavenly inspiration. Then I received a grace which I have always looked upon as one of the greatest in my life [. . .]. I considered that I was born for *glory* and when I searched out the means of attaining it, God inspired in me the sentiments I have just described. He made me understand my own *glory* would not be evident to the eyes of mortals, that it would consist in becoming a great *saint!* This desire could certainly appear daring if one were to consider how weak and imperfect I was, and how, after seven years in the religious life, I still am weak and imperfect. I always feel, however, the same bold confidence [*confiance*] of becoming a great saint because I don't count on my merits

> since I have *none*, but I trust in Him who is Virtue and Holiness. God alone, content with my weak efforts, will raise me to Himself and make me a *saint*, clothing me in His infinite merits.[32]

Thérèse had desired, since her adolescence, to become a great saint; it was God who had placed this desire in her heart. Yet, how to do so? Thérèse admitted that, after seven years of religious life, she was still "weak and imperfect." In that same period of time (late 1894), Thérèse and her family members started to realize that her fragile health may have lead Thérèse to an early death. How could Thérèse reach her goal of becoming a great saint in a short amount of time, and being still so "weak and imperfect"?

Through God's Word, she finds the answer: "The elevator which must raise me to heaven is Your arms, O Jesus! And for this I had no need to grow up, but rather I had to remain *little* and become this more and more."[33]

---

[32] Autobiographical Manuscript dedicated to Mother Agnes of Jesus, in *Story of a Soul: The Autobiography of Saint Thérèse of Lisieux*, trans. John Clarke, OCD, study ed. Marc Foley, OCD (Washington, D.C.: ICS Publications, 2019).

[33] Autobiographical Manuscript dedicated to Mother Marie de Gonzague, in *Story of a Soul: The Autobiography*

Thérèse underwent a long and intense journey, even though her life was abbreviated by tuberculosis into just 24 years. A life of hidden suffering, a life of hidden sacrifice, but most of all a life of peace, joy, and love (for both God and for neighbor). The foundations for her "Little Way" were set out by God Himself, through her parents,[34] and her family, and through many other influences and sources. The main source and influence, however, of Thérèse's "Little Way" was most certainly the Holy Scriptures, both in the Old and New Testaments, especially the prophet Isaiah, the Book of Proverbs, and the Gospels. But it was the author of the Holy Scriptures, that is, the Holy Spirit Himself, together with Jesus, Thérèse's "Spouse,"

---

of Saint Thérèse of Lisieux, trans. John Clarke, OCD, study ed. Marc Foley, OCD (Washington, D.C.: ICS Publications, 2019).

[34] Joseph Spence, "Dio Padre nell'esperienza e nella teologia di santa Teresa di Lisieux: un segno di speranza per il mondo di oggi" ["God the Father in the Experience and the Theology of Saint Thérèse of Lisieux: A Sign of Hope for the World Today"], in *Ripensare la teologia con santa Teresa di Lisieux: Atti del Seminario di approfondimento (Pontificia Facoltà Teologica Teresianum, Roma, 23–24 maggio 2024)*, ed. L. Strzyz-Steinert, *Theologie der Spiritualität. Quellen und Studien* 14 (Sankt Ottilien, Germany: EOS Verlag, 2025), 149–64.

who were instructing her in the depths of her heart, and whispering to her the secrets of God's tender and compassionate love and mercy. The Holy Spirit was teaching her the confidence—the *confiance*—and the trusting abandonment and self-surrender, to God, that true children of God the Father must have. The secrets of the love between the Father and the Son, revealed to us by Jesus and related in the Gospels, are the same secrets that God "revealed" once again to Thérèse, in an historical period and context in which those "secrets" had been forgotten, or rather, smothered by human fear and misconception (e.g., Jansenism). Thérèse, guided by the Holy Spirit, the true Author of the Scriptures, has helped modern-day man to "dust off" the Holy Scriptures and to penetrate their true meaning, as well as one of their most fundamental messages, which Jesus Himself revealed to us: God is a loving Father.

St. Thérèse of the Child Jesus and of the Holy Face (June 7, 1897). This picture was taken by her sister Céline (Sr. Geneviève of the Holy Face). Thérèse is holding an image that she herself had made and kept in her breviary, of the Child Jesus and of the Holy Face (of Tours).

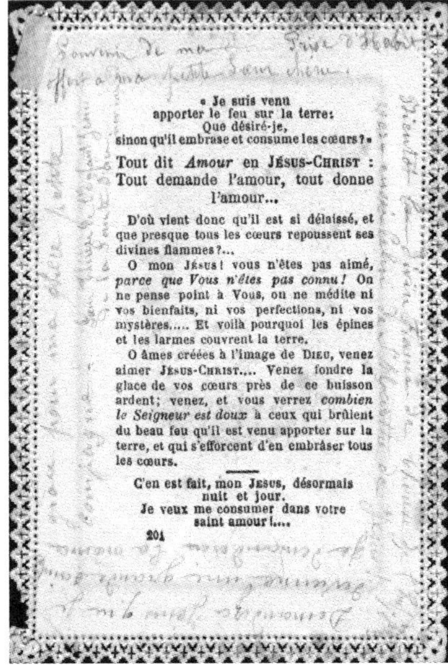

« Je suis venu
apporter le feu sur la terre:
Que désiré-je,
sinon qu'il embrase et consume les cœurs? »

Tout dit *Amour* en Jésus-Christ :
Tout demande l'amour, tout donne
l'amour...

D'où vient donc qu'il est si délaissé, et que presque tous les cœurs repoussent ses divines flammes?...

O mon Jésus! vous n'êtes pas aimé, *parce que Vous n'êtes pas connu!* On ne pense point à Vous, on ne médite ni vos bienfaits, ni vos perfections, ni vos mystères..... Et voilà pourquoi les épines et les larmes couvrent la terre.

O âmes créées à l'image de Dieu, venez aimer Jésus-Christ.... Venez fondre la glace de vos cœurs près de ce buisson ardent; venez, et vous verrez *combien le Seigneur est doux* à ceux qui brûlent du beau feu qu'il est venu apporter sur la terre, et qui s'efforcent d'en embrâser tous les cœurs.

C'en est fait, mon Jésus, désormais
nuit et jour.
Je veux me consumer dans votre
saint amour!....

201

Above: Holy card that Thérèse gave to Sr. Martha on the day of her own Clothing Ceremony (January 10, 1889).

Below: Close-up image of Thérèse's signature. Thérèse chose to add "of the Holy Face" to her religious name for her Clothing Ceremony. This holy card bears the first signature of Thérèse using her whole (new) religious name: Sœur Thérèse de l'Enfant-Jésus de la Sainte-Face.

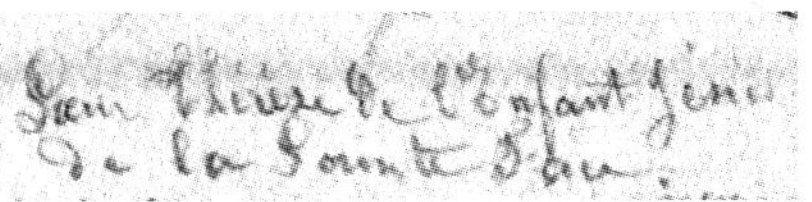

CHAPTER TWO

St. Thérèse's Experience of the Mysteries of the Child Jesus and of the Holy Face of Jesus

1. Introduction: some historical and theological background

Sister Thérèse of the Child Jesus and of the Holy Face: Thus the name chosen by sixteen-year-old Thérèse on the day she took her habit, January 10, 1889. Her first signature with her full name is precisely from that day, the day of her Vestition, on the back of a holy card given to Sr. Martha (*LT* 80). On the front of the holy card, an image of the Child Jesus in His cradle, already contemplating the cross, with the words: "*Pater, fiat voluntas tua,*" "Father, may Your will be done." This image, offered by Thérèse to her nun-sister Martha of Jesus, is a sort of synthesis of Thérèse's religious name and, I would say, of her spirituality. The two mysteries of Christ, especially chosen and contemplated by Thérèse, both focus on Jesus's humility, abasement, and *kenosis*. As Thérèse would later write in the first pages of her *Story of a Soul*:

> In fact, since the nature of love is to humble oneself (*de s'abaisser*), if all souls resembled those of the holy doctors [. . .], it seems God would not descend so low when coming to their heart. But He created the child who knows only how to make his feeble cries heard; He has created the poor savage who has nothing but the natural law to guide him. It is to their hearts that God deigns to lower Himself (*s'abaisser*).[35]

It is Christ's *kenosis*, then, that forms the theological root and principle underlying Thérèse's "Little Way." As God chose to humble and to abase Himself (*s'abaisser*), in the *kenosis* of Christ's Incarnation and Cross, we too—Thérèse found—must humble and abase ourselves so that God can manifest His mercy

---

35 Autobiographical Manuscript dedicated to Mother Agnes of Jesus, in *Story of a Soul: The Autobiography of Saint Thérèse of Lisieux*, trans. John Clarke, OCD, study ed. Marc Foley, OCD (Washington, D.C.: ICS Publications, 2019).

and His goodness, and stoop down to gather us up. "The elevator which must raise me to heaven is Your arms, O Jesus! And for this I had no need to grow up, but rather I had to remain *little* and become this more and more" (Ms C, 3r°), Thérèse would later write. If God's *kenosis*, in Christ, is the root of Thérèse's "Little Way." it is also the theological root of her devotion to the mysteries of the Child Jesus and the Holy Face. Christ's Incarnation and His Paschal Mystery—the two most fundamental mysteries of our faith, together with that of the Most Holy Trinity—are the two mysteries that Thérèse contemplates in her devotion to the Child Jesus and to the Holy Face of Jesus.

Having said this on a theological level, let's try to narrow in on Thérèse's life experience to better understand how she discovered these devotions and, more importantly, how she lived them. In Thérèse's case, as a matter of fact, her religious name was not simply nominal—excuse the pun. It was of fundamental importance for her spirituality and is, again, a synthesis of her spirituality.

2. The historical roots of the devotion to the Child Jesus in France

Both devotions were extremely popular and well-known during Thérèse's time. She did not invent them, of course—she received them. In a way, she "breathed" them in. However, she also produced a personal synthesis of the two devotions, with a unique and original meaning and interpretation.

The first of the two mysteries that attracted Thérèse and she with which came into contact was that of the Child Jesus. Being a child, in fact, and the smallest of the family, Thérèse's sisters, and relatives, and friends would tendentially use the image of the Child Jesus when speaking to Thérèse about God.

Besides being a fundamental mystery of our faith, as seen in the Gospel of Matthew and especially in the picturesque narrations of Luke, the devotion to the Child Jesus had "exploded" onto the scene of the Church in France in the 17th century. In 1630, Margaret Parigot, an orphan who had lost her mother, entered the Carmel of Beaune, in East-Central France, at only eleven years old. At sixteen, she consecrated herself to God as a Carmelite. The Child Jesus appeared to her, teaching her to honor and venerate Him in a particular way from the time of His Incarnation to His twelfth year of age: the Child Jesus, precisely. This apparition inspired Sr. Margaret of the Holy Sacrament to create a devotional Rosary with fifteen beads: on the first three beads, the devotee would pray three Our Fathers, in honor of Jesus, Mary, and Joseph; and, with the remaining twelve beads, would pray Hail Mary's to honor the first twelve years of Jesus's childhood. In the year 1637, Sr. Margaret was asked to pray that the Queen of France, Anne of Austria, might conceive an heir to the throne. Before the Queen herself had realized that she was pregnant, near December 15, 1637, Sr. Margaret informed her Prioress that the queen would give birth to her heir (King Louis XIV of France). The queen came to know of Sr. Margaret's prophecy and, to thank her for her prayers, sent to the Carmel a statue of King Louis XIV as a child. In another apparition to Sr. Margaret, the Child Jesus requested that she have a chapel constructed in His honor, which was built and inaugurated on December 25, 1639. The apparitions of the Child Jesus to Sr. Margaret of the Holy Sacrament; her Rosary dedicated to the Child Jesus; her prayers for the heir of Queen Anne; and the chapel built in honor of the Child Jesus, all contributed to a growing devotion to the Child Jesus in France, and, in a particular way, in the Carmels across France. Sr. Margaret of the Holy Sacrament, in fact, was a Carmelite.[36] The Infant Jesus of Prague, which also became famous in the 17th Century, due once more to a Carmelite influence—Father

---

36 *Sainte Thérèse de Lisieux: La vie en images*, ed. P. Descouvemont, H. N. Loose, and D. Leprince (Paris: Cerf, 1995), 132–33.

Cyril of the Mother of God, a Carmelite friar—was also a highly spread and popular devotion at the time of Thérèse and in particular among Carmelites. Furthermore, St. Teresa of Avila also had a great devotion to the Child Jesus, and it was well known how she would bring a statue of the Child Jesus to each of the convents that she founded. Likewise, Venerable Anne of Jesus, for the foundation of the first Carmel in Paris, the "Carmel of the Incarnation," brought a statue of the Child Jesus to the monastery.[37] No surprise, then, to find such a strong devotion to the Child Jesus in France and especially in Carmels at the end of the 19th century, during Thérèse's time. A quick glance at the *numerous* statues of the Child Jesus present in the Lisieux Carmel during Thérèse's time testifies to this fact.[38]

3. Devotion to the Child Jesus in the Martin family and in Thérèse

The devotion to the Child Jesus in France was strong, then, at Thérèse's time; and in the Martin family, especially when addressing the "baby" of the family, Thérèse, it was of common usage. All of this was not indifferent to Thérèse: she often speaks of the Child

[37] *Sainte Thérèse de Lisieux: La vie en images*, 131.

[38] See the Lisieux Carmel Archives website.

Jesus in her first *Letters*, as a matter of fact. And in the Carmelite monasteries of France, in particular, the devotion to the Child Jesus was especially strong. These historical backgrounds help us to understand the desire and the inspiration that were happily and providentially shared by Thérèse and the Prioress of Carmel in the choice of Thérèse's name. The Prioress, Mother Marie de Gonzague, had learned from Pauline (Sr. Agnes of Jesus) of Thérèse's desire to enter Carmel. In October of 1882, shortly after Pauline's entrance into the Lisieux Carmel, Thérèse (then nine years old) made a visit to her and to the other Carmelite nuns for the first time. She would later recount this providential meeting with the Prioress in her *Manuscript* A:

> While speaking about the visit to the Carmelites, I am reminded of the first visit which took place shortly after Pauline's entrance [. . .]. The morning of the day I was to visit, I was thinking things over in my *bed* [. . .], I wondered what name I would be given in Carmel. I knew there was a Sister Thérèse of Jesus; however, my beautiful name of Thérèse could not be taken away from me. All of a sudden, I thought of *Little* Jesus whom I loved

> so much, and I said: "Oh! how happy I would be if they called me Thérèse of the Child Jesus!" I *said nothing* during the visit about the *dream* I had while wide awake. But to good *Mother Marie de Gonzague*, who was asking the sisters what name I should be given, came the idea of calling me by the name I had *dreamed* about. My joy was great and this happy meeting of minds seemed to be a singular favor from my beloved Child Jesus.[39]

We've already seen in our last Chapter, on Thérèse's "Little Way," how Thérèse's devotion to the Child Jesus was not limited to her earliest years of life. On her pilgrimage to Rome, Thérèse often evokes the image of the "little ball" or "little toy" of Jesus (which was she herself), whom the Child Jesus must feel free to play with according to His whims and to His will. Thérèse's devotion to the Child Jesus would never fade with the passage of time, because her devotion was not a "childish" one. Rather, it was a devotion to Christ

---

39 Autobiographical Manuscript dedicated to Mother Agnes of Jesus, in *Story of a Soul: The Autobiography of Saint Thérèse of Lisieux*, trans. John Clarke, OCD, study ed. Marc Foley, OCD (Washington, D.C.: ICS Publications, 2019).

as seen in one of His most fundamental mysteries and characteristics: His Incarnation. Thérèse, years later, would attribute to the Child Jesus the grace of her "complete conversion" on Christmas Eve 1886, when the "gentle, *little* Child of only one hour, changed the night of my soul into rays of light." Even her "wedding day" to Jesus, the day of her Profession at age seventeen (September 8, 1890), Thérèse would later describe in reference to the Child Jesus:

> Mary's nativity! What a beautiful feast on which to become the spouse of Jesus! It was the *little* Blessed Virgin, one day old, who was presenting her *little* flower to the *little* Jesus. Everything was little that day except the graces and the peace I received.[40]

4. The historical background to the devotion for the Holy Face of Jesus in France

Let's switch perspective now from Thérèse's experience of the mystery of the Child Jesus to that of the Holy Face. As I mentioned earlier, in reality, the two

---

[40] *Story of a Soul*, trans. John Clarke, OCD, study ed. Marc Foley, OCD, "Autobiographical Manuscript dedicated to Mother Agnes of Jesus."

mysteries are strictly connected. And Thérèse had no difficulty in associating them. This was true not only because of her quick and penetrating theological insight into the mysteries of the life of Christ, but it was also actually a common association of Catholic piety at the time, as seen by the holy card that Thérèse gave to Sr. Martha on the day of her own Vestition ceremony (January 10, 1889). Let's take a quick glance at some other holy cards that Thérèse received in her childhood years, available for further review on the Carmel of Lisieux Archives website.[41]

[41] Carmel of Lisieux Archives, "Images liées à l'enfance," accessed March 27, 2025, https://archives.carmeldelisieux.fr/en/la-vie-de-sainte-therese-de-lisieux/images-offertes-a-therese/images-liees-a-lenfance/

As you can see, the Child Jesus was often portrayed with an explicit allusion to the Cross, either at His feet or even on His shoulders.

It's worth mentioning, at this point, the historical background that helps to understand the devotion to the Holy Face in France at that time. The devotion to the Holy Face quickly spread through France only about thirty years before Thérèse's birth. This spread is tied mainly to three decisive influences: Sr. Mary of Saint Peter; Mr. Léon Dupont; and a miraculous event at St. Peter's Basilica in Rome. Sr. Mary of St. Peter entered the Carmel of Tours in 1839. In 1843, she received "messages" from the Lord, requesting her to contribute toward the reparation for sinners' blasphemies and profanation of the Holy Day of Obligation (Sundays). She wrote, in that sense, a Litany of twenty-four invocations to the Holy Name of God. In 1845, the Lord invited her to start venerating His Holy Face. The nun desired to become like a new Veronica, to console the humiliated Face of the Lord, and to obtain the conversion of sinners in France. Contemporarily, in the city of Tours, Mr. Léon Dupont was working in the same direction, propagating the Holy Name of God. On the Feast of the Epiphany in the year 1849, at St. Peter's Basilica, during the public veneration of the Veil of Veronica (present in Rome since at least the 1200s), the veil was suddenly flooded with light coming from within itself (and not from any external sources). The prodigious event lasted for three hours, while the people came in amazement to see it. An apostolic notary lawyer wrote down the happening and brought the news to the pope. The news spread quickly. Mr. Léon Dupont soon heard of the miraculous event and became a devotee of the Veil of Veronica. He would spend the rest of his life propagating the devotion to the Holy Face as represented in the Veil of Veronica. After his death, his living room, where flocks of people had passed through over the years to venerate his copy of the Veil of Veronica—which had in the meantime become famous as being a miraculous image—that same living room was transformed into a chapel: the *Oratoire de la Saint-Face*, in Tours, which soon became a destination for pilgrims. Only a few months after Mr. Léon Dupont's death, the Confraternity of the Holy Face was founded in Tours.[42]

[42] *Sainte Thérèse de Lisieux: La vie en images*, ed. P. Descouvemont, H. N. Loose, and D. Leprince (Paris: Cerf, 1995), 174.

5. Devotion to the Holy Face in the Martin family and in Thérèse

Mother Geneviève, one of the founders of the Lisieux Carmel in 1838, devoted herself to the Holy Face. Therefore, the Lisieux Carmel collaborated for the foundation of a Confraternity of the Holy Face in Lisieux; on April 26, 1885, Louis Martin and four of his daughters—Thérèse included—enrolled in the Confraternity of the Holy Face.[43] Thérèse was twelve years old.

Thérèse was, then, devoted to the Holy Face from at least the age of twelve. In fact, she also painted a copy of the Veil of Veronica and had it placed in the arbor or gazebo in the backyard of *Les Buissonnets*, the Martins' home in Lisieux. In December of 1889, once *Les Buissonnets* had been sold, the painting was taken to the Lisieux Carmel and placed into another gazebo, called the "Hermitage of the Holy Face."

In the Lisieux Carmel, Mother Geneviève—whom Thérèse got to know and for whom she had much veneration until her holy death—had started the custom of having the novices read the life of Sr. Mary of St. Peter. And so, Pauline (Sr. Agnes of Jesus) introduced Thérèse more fully into the mystery of the Holy Face,

---

43 *Sainte Thérèse de Lisieux: La vie en images*, 162.

having her read the life of Sr. Mary of St. Peter, and even instructing her on the devotion to the Holy Face and its biblical roots in the Psalms, in reference to the many Psalms that speak of longing to see God's Face.[44]

6. A turning point in Thérèse's devotion to the Holy Face

Yet, Thérèse's personal "encounter" with the Holy Face came about not only—or not primarily—because of Pauline's instructions, but because of another series of events: her father's illness. Louis Martin had been showing worrisome signs in regard to his mental health. On June 23, 1888, Louis Martin suddenly disappeared and was found four days later in another town, Le Havre. On February 12, 1889, the unthinkable occurred: hallucinating and convinced that a battle was raging in Lisieux, Mr. Martin took out his revolver in an attempt to defend his two daughters, Céline and Léonie, and the servant Marie Cosseron. They quickly sought help from their Uncle Isidore Guérin, who then fetched a strong, tall friend to come and calm Louis Martin. They took him on "a walk" to the Lisieux Carmel to say goodbye. He brought a few small fish in a handkerchief and gave them to Pauline.

---

[44] *Sainte Thérèse de Lisieux: La vie en images*, 166.

They then took him immediately to the psychiatric ward in the *Bon Saveur* hospital in Caen. He was to remain there for thirty-nine long months. Mr. Martin suffered from cerebral arteriosclerosis; he would later be confined to a wheelchair. Thérèse later wrote, in her *Manuscript* A: "Ah! that day, I didn't say I was able to suffer more! Words cannot express our anguish, and I'm not going to attempt to describe it."[45] Thérèse, instructed by Pauline (Sr. Agnes of Jesus) in the devotion to the Holy Face as a novice, had thus chosen this mystery as a complementary addition to her religious name on the day of her Vestition (January 10, 1889); the mystery of Christ's suffering had been a refuge for her in the humiliating and anguishing months of their dear father Louis' downturn in his mental health. Only a month after her Clothing Ceremony, Louis was interned in the *Bon Sauveur* Hospital. In the following months and years, the Holy Face of Jesus would be the source of a constant spiritual strength and comfort for Thérèse. And an explanation, on a spiritual level, of her father's humiliation and sufferings: Jesus was associating him and their whole family to His own humiliation and sufferings, as contemplated in His

[45] *Story of a Soul*, trans. John Clarke, OCD, study ed. Marc Foley, OCD, "Autobiographical Manuscript dedicated to Mother Agnes of Jesus," 73r°.

Holy Face. On Louis Martin's funeral holy card, in fact, his daughters chose the image of the Holy Face.

7. Two "beacons" in a time of darkness: St. John of the Cross and the Holy Face of Jesus

Thérèse, in the time of her father's illness, sought light and inspiration. It was at that time that she would borrow from the Carmel library the *Spiritual Canticle* and *Living Flame of Love* of St. John of the Cross, who would soon become an inseparable companion and guide on her spiritual journey. At the same time, it was in the Holy Face of Jesus that Thérèse found light and consolation. Sr. Agnes of Jesus (Pauline) testified, years later, in the Process for Thérèse's beatification:

> Devotion to the Holy Face was the special attraction of the Servant of God. However tender her devotion to the Child Jesus, it cannot be compared to her devotion to the Holy Face. It was in Carmel, at the time of our great trials in connection with our father's cerebral illness, that she became more attached to the mystery of the Passion, and it was then that she

> obtained the right to add to her name that of the Holy Face.[46]

In May of 1890, Céline went on a pilgrimage with her Aunt, Uncle, and cousins, Jeanne and Marie Guérin, to Lourdes and Tours. Upon her return, she gave an image with the photograph of the *Oratoire de la Saint-Face*, in Tours, to Thérèse.[47] It was only in July of 1890, however, a few months before her Profession, that Thérèse found a Biblical reference and content, as it were, to her devotion to the Holy Face. She wrote about it in ecstatic terms to her pen-pal and confidant, Céline, with whom she had shared her sufferings and her inspirations regarding their dear father Louis's sickness since the beginning. In her *Letter* 108, on July 18, 1890, Thérèse wrote:

---

[46] Carmel of Lisieux Archives, "Les témoignages du procès apostolique – Témoin 6: Agnès de Jésus, O.C.D.," accessed March 27, 2025, https://archives.carmeldelisieux.fr/en/naissance-dune-sainte/les-proces-la-sainte-de-therese/le-proces-apostolique/les-temoignages-du-proces-apostolique/#temoin-6-agnes-de-jesus-o-c-d. (Translation slightly adjusted by the author from the original French testimony on the same website.)

[47] *Sainte Thérèse de Lisieux: La vie en images*, 158–59.

Céline, it's *such a long time ago* . . . and already the soul of the prophet Isaiah was immersed, just as our own soul is, in the HIDDEN BEAUTIES of Jesus [. . .]. Céline, since Jesus was (alone in treading the wine) which He is giving us to drink, let us not refuse in our turn to wear clothing stained in blood . . . let us tread for Jesus a new wine which may quench His thirst, which will return Him love for love [. . .]. His face was though as hidden! . . . Céline, it is still hidden today, for who understands the tears of Jesus? [. . .]. Papa! . . . Ah, Céline, I cannot tell you all I am thinking, it would take too long, and how to say things that the mind itself can hardly express, deep things that are in the innermost recesses of the soul! . . . Jesus has sent us the best chosen Cross that He was able to find in His immense love . . . how can we complain when He Himself was looked upon as a man struck by God and humbled![48]

---

48 *General Correspondence, Vol. I,* trans. John Clarke, OCD, 108.

Together with her *Letter* 108, in which she quotes the Prophet Isaiah, Thérèse attached a page with various passages of the Prophet Isaiah copied on it. "I'm sending you a page which says much to my soul," she wrote at the beginning of her *Letter* 108. It seems that Thérèse had already copied this page for her personal meditation prior to writing to Céline. They are excerpts from the Prophet Isaiah, chapters 53 and 63. In reality, it seems that Thérèse copied them from the readings of the Liturgy of the Hours, celebrated in Lent.[49]

8. Thérèse's art: a reflection of her interior contemplation

Let's skip now to the year 1894, shortly after Louis Martin's death. A few years before, Pauline had painted a holy card for Céline: a lily sustaining the Veil of Veronica. The flower of the lily represented Céline, who had remained close to their father to aid him in his sickness; the stem represented their mother Zélie; the thorns represented their father in his sickness; and the four buds their four deceased siblings. Thérèse, shortly after Louis Martin's death, and inspired by the

[49] St. Thérèse of Lisieux, *General Correspondence*, vol. 1: *1887–1890*, 631–35.

holy card painted by Pauline, painted herself something quite similar: a chasuble, destined for use in the celebration of the Holy Mass. The two roses represent her parents, Louis and Zélie. The five lilies represent the five Martin daughters; the four buds, represented their four deceased siblings. The lily that Thérèse painted to represent herself is the one seen on the left, half-hidden behind the Face of Jesus.

9. Thérèse and the Holy Face of Jesus

Turning now toward the conclusion of this chapter, let us reassume the main steps of Thérèse's devotion to the Holy Face. Between 1895–1896, Thérèse wrote her briefest prayer, *Prayer* 11: "Make me resemble you, Jesus!" She wrote it around a stamp of the Holy Face of Tours. She kept this parchment in a little pouch on her heart, together with her Profession Note, the Creed, written in her own blood, and some relics: the last tear of Mother Geneviève, as well as some hair of Sr. Marie of Saint Peter, and the Gospels, of course.[50] On August 12, 1895, Thérèse composed her *Poem* 20, "My Heaven on Earth," a Canticle to the Holy Face: "Jesus, your ineffable image is the star that guides my steps. Ah! you know, your sweet Face is for me Heaven on earth." On August 6, 1896, together with her two novices, Céline (Sr. Geneviève of the Holy Face) and Sr. Marie of the Trinity, Thérèse consecrated herself to the Holy Face (*Prayer* 12).[51] Thérèse's holy death took

---

[50] See *Thérèse et Lisieux*, photographs by H. N. Loose, text by P. Descouvemont, presentation by D. Leprince (Paris: Cerf, 1991), 139.

[51] It's also worth mentioning that Céline Martin (Sr. Geneviève of the Holy Face) painted, in the year 1904, a beautiful image of the Holy Face of Jesus, basing herself on the Shroud of Turin; the Shroud became world-famous after the photograph taken by Secondo Pia in Turin in May of 1898, less than a year after Thérèse's death. In the year 1909, Céline Martin (Sr. Geneviève of the Holy Face) won the *Grand Prix* of the International Exposition of Religious Arts in Holland. For more information, see biographical notes in *Thérèse et Lisieux* (Paris: Cerf, 1991).

place while gazing at her Crucifix, with the image of the Holy Face of Tours pinned to her bed curtain.

St. Thérèse (together with the other nuns of the monastery) hugging the Crucifix in the Courtyard of the Lisieux Carmel (June 1896).

CHAPTER THREE

Jesus as Spouse and Thérèse

1. Introduction: "Jesus is my only love!"

"Jesus is my only love!" ("*Jésus est mon unique Amour!*") Some scholars say that this phrase of Thérèse is a sort of synthesis of Thérèse's entire spirituality. I agree. I would also add that—even if it were not to sum up all of her spirituality—it is certainly a summary of her spousal relationship with Jesus. Thérèse engraved this phrase—*Jésus est mon unique Amour!*—into the wood of the left-hand frame of the door of her cell.[52] It was

[52] Perhaps Thérèse was inspired, in this, by *Deuteronomy* 6:5–9, which was often read in the Liturgy of the Hours even in her time: "Love the LORD your God with all your heart and with all your soul and with all your strength. These commandments that I give you today are to be on your hearts. Impress them on your children. Talk about them when you sit at home and when you walk along the

the third and last cell she lived in at the Lisieux Carmel (besides the Infirmary of course, in the last months of her life). She moved into her third cell in August of 1894, so certainly this inscription is subsequent to that date.[53] Fr. Pierre Descouvemont—one of the greatest scholars of Thérèse—retains that she probably wrote this phrase around June of 1897, a few months before her death. We must remember that Thérèse was suffering terribly, not only physically, but also spiritually (and, consequently, psychologically). She was in the midst of her trial against faith: more specifically, the trial of faith in the existence of Heaven, as she confided to Pauline: "Ah! but I really believe in the Thief [Jesus]! It's upon heaven that everything bears. How strange and incomprehensible it is!"[54] It was during

---

road, when you lie down and when you get up. Tie them as symbols on your hands and bind them on your foreheads. Write them on the doorframes of your houses and on your gates." (See: https://archives.carmeldelisieux.fr/en/oeuvres-de-therese/ecrits-divers/jesus-est-mon-unique-amour/. Accessed on March 27, 2025).

[53] Carmel of Lisieux Archives, "Jésus est mon unique amour," accessed March 27, 2025, https://archives.carmeldelisieux.fr/en/oeuvres-de-therese/ecrits-divers/jesus-est-mon-unique-amour/

[54] St. Thérèse of Lisieux, *Yellow Notebook*, 7.2.3 (July 2, 1897, third statement).

this time of intense spiritual darkness and struggle, from Easter 1896 till her very death, that Thérèse made some bold and surprising gestures of faith. For example, she wrote the Creed in her own blood. And, in June of 1897, she scribbled on a scrap piece of paper: "My God, with the help of your grace, I am ready to shed all my blood for each of the articles of the Symbol [Creed]." Probably in the same time period, June of 1897, she also wrote this synthetic and powerful statement, carving it into the wood of her doorframe: *Jésus est mon unique Amour!* It's one of those things that Thérèse should not have done, according to the rules of the monastery. But she did it anyway.

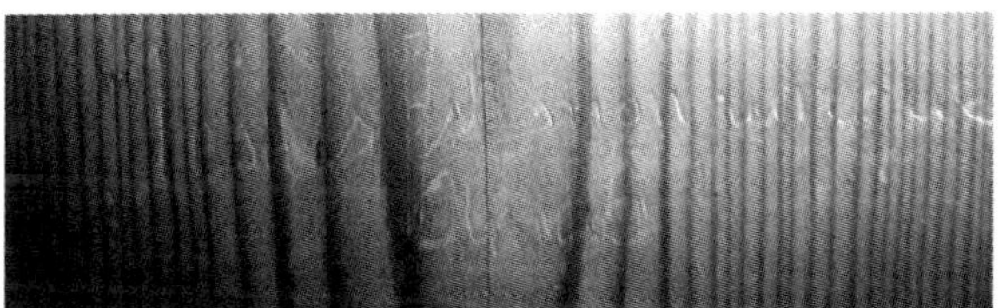

The engraving of Thérèse on the left-hand side of the doorframe of her cell in the Lisieux Carmel: "Jésus est mon unique Amour" ("Jesus is my only Love"). © Archives du Carmel de Lisieux. Used with permission.

2. The concept of Jesus as Spouse in religious life at the time

It must be said from the beginning of this chapter that the fact of retaining Jesus as her Spouse was certainly not an invention of Thérèse. It was not an original experience. All nuns at that time considered themselves as brides of Jesus. It was common knowledge, common usage, common language. And, in reality . . . they weren't wrong. At this point, there is no time to go into the many Biblical and Patristic texts—such as St. Ambrose or Origen's commentaries on the Song of Songs—that could further illustrate this point. We cannot, here, explore in depth the Scriptural and Patristic foundations for understanding God as Spouse. That could be the subject of an entire chapter or even an entire book. Most certainly, God is a Spouse, as John's visions recounted in the Book of Revelation convey:

> I saw the Holy City, the new Jerusalem, coming down out of heaven from God, prepared as a bride beautifully dressed for her husband [. . .]. Come, I will show you the bride, the wife of the Lamb. And he carried me away in the Spirit to a mountain great and high, and showed me the

> Holy City, Jerusalem, coming down out of heaven from God (Rev. 21:2; 9b–10).

All men and women, and especially all Christians, are "brides" prepared and beautifully dressed for our "husband," the Bridegroom Jesus, the Lamb who was slain and now stands at the center of the throne (cf. Revelation 5). Thus, it is with Baptism, especially, that we are consecrated and become "brides" of the Bridegroom Jesus; and all those who live a special consecration to God in the Church—for example, nuns like Thérèse herself—are "brides" inasmuch as they are Christians in the first place. They express and live out in a special way that "being brides," which all Christians are meant to live.

So, if Thérèse's experience of Jesus as Spouse was not original, in and of itself, what was original about it?

3. The spousal love of Jesus as lived and expressed in the Martin family

First of all, Thérèse had the unique experience of having two parents (now canonized) who fondly and deeply loved one another: "God gave me a father and a mother more worthy of heaven than of earth," Thérèse would later write to Fr. Bellière (cf. LT 261). Even though her mother Zélie died when she was only four years old, Thérèse still had many precious and fond memories of her dear mother. Psychologists often speak of the importance of having parents who love one another for a healthy development of an infant's psyche, above and beyond conscious memories. Therefore, Thérèse had a living and extraordinary example, in her holy parents, of what it means as a couple to live one's spousal love in everyday life.

Most certainly, this family environment helped Thérèse, consciously or unconsciously, to live a balanced and passionate love for Jesus. Thérèse also knew, from her own family experience, that spousal love and affection generate life: she was the last of nine children, in fact. The spiritual tie between spousal love for Jesus and becoming a mother of souls (which we'll be speaking about it in our next chapter as well) probably came naturally to Thérèse, considering her holy parents' espousal love and the many children they had.

4. Thérèse's experience of Jesus as her "Fiancé"

Let's move on now to Thérèse's personal experience. I would say that the first strong and explicitly "spousal" experience or encounter with Jesus that Thérèse had was on the day of her First Communion. Even in this experience, Thérèse was taken and led by the popular devotion and spirituality of her time. Mother Marie de Gonzague had given Thérèse a holy card in preparation for her First Communion. It depicts a young Shepherd (Jesus) kissing the forehead of a young shepherdess. The poem on the back of the holy card recounts the story of their chaste love. Also on the day of Thérèse's First Communion, she received a holy card from Fr. Almire Pichon, SJ—who would later become her spiritual director in Carmel—depicting Jesus holding a ciborium and giving His enflamed, Sacred Heart to a child girl on the day of her First Communion. In the holy cards found among the images in the Lisieux Carmel, used during Thérèse's time to make cards or to use as models for paintings, another holy card was found (which Thérèse may or may not have seen): it portrays Jesus kissing a young girl on the forehead, with His right hand behind her head, as He holds a ciborium with the Eucharist in His left hand (See image below).[55]

[55] *Sainte Thérèse de Lisieux: La vie en images*, ed. P. Descouvemont, H. N. Loose, and D. Leprince (Paris: Cerf, 1995), 60.

DILECTUS MEUS MIHI ET EGO ILLI

Avec l'Amante des Cantiques,
O Bien-Aimé, je désire ardemment
Votre chaste baiser, vos caresses mystiques;
Je soupire toujours après l'heureux moment
Où je pourrai par votre Eucharistie,
M'unir étroitement à Vous,
Jésus-Amour! Jésus-Hostie!
Père, Ami, Frère, tendre Epoux!

Mon âme est votre Epouse…
O mon Jésus, mon doux Sauveur,
De vos faveurs elle est jalouse,
Votre amour est tout son bonheur.

De votre Cœur tout brûlant qui nous aime,
Oh! n'est-ce point le but suprême?
Ah! vous quittez les Cieux
Pour notre pauvre terre,
O Prisonnier du Sanctuaire,
Afin de nous offrir ce baiser précieux!

Devant tant de bonheur, mon âme anéantie
Ne sait plus que redire en contemplant l'hostie…
« A moi ce céleste baiser!
« Ma soif d'amour, seul il peut l'apaiser…
« Plus rien ici-bas ne me touche,
« Je suis à l'Epoux immortel!
« Ah! qu'il me donne un baiser de sa bouche,
« Mon Bien-Aimé, le Captif de l'Autel! »

L'instant divin entre Dieu et l'Âme.

The popular devotion and spirituality, then, helped Thérèse to understand the spousal dimension of the Eucharist, or Communion (with Jesus). In fact, years later, in her *Manuscript* A, Thérèse recounted the experience of her First Communion in terms of a spousal encounter with Jesus. She wrote:

> Ah! how sweet was that first kiss of Jesus! It was a kiss of love; I *felt* that *I was loved*, and I said: "I love You, and I give myself to You forever!" There were no demands made, no struggles, no sacrifices; for

> a long time now Jesus and poor little Thérèse *looked* at and understood each other. That day, it was no longer simply a *look*, it was a fusion; they were no longer two, Thérèse had vanished as a drop of water is lost in the immensity of the ocean. Jesus alone remained; He was the Master, the King. Had not Thérèse asked Him to take away her *liberty*, for her *liberty* frightened her? She felt so feeble and fragile that she wanted to be united forever to the divine Strength! Her joy was too great, too deep for her to contain, and tears of consolation soon flowed, to the great consternation of her companions [. . .]. They did not understand that all the joy of Heaven having entered my heart, this exiled heart was unable to bear it without shedding tears.

This unforgettable experience, of the "first kiss of Jesus," remained with Thérèse her whole life. Sr. Mary of the Trinity later testified for the process of Thérèse's beatification:

> [Thérèse] had a burning desire for holy communion; the inability to receive it

> daily was the greatest suffering she had to endure. She would have suffered anything rather than miss going to Holy Communion. One communion day she was very ill and had been ordered to take some medicine. Now it was customary here to miss Holy Communion because of that. Faced with this dilemma Sister Thérèse broke down and cried, but she pleaded her cause so ably with Mother Prioress that not only was she allowed to postpone the medicine until after Mass, but from that day on the custom of missing Holy Communion in such cases was abolished.[56]

We must remember how rampant the pseudo-spirituality of Jansenism was in France and even in the Lisieux Carmel at that time. Jansenism, along with Mother Marie de Gonzague's strange and arbitrary customs, limited the nuns from receiving Communion every day. They would receive two or three times a week. Thérèse, when she wrote those lines regarding

---

[56] *St. Thérèse of Lisieux by Those Who Knew Her: Testimonies from the Process of Beatification*, ed. C. O'Mahony (Dublin: Veritas Publications, 2015), 232–33.

her First Communion, was twenty-two years old. For this young woman, totally in love with Jesus, receiving Holy Communion was like receiving a (chaste) kiss from her Beloved, Jesus. "Thérèse had a burning desire for holy communion," Sr. Mary of the Trinity related.

5. Some anthropological and theological clarifications

We must not be confused, however. Thérèse's experience of Jesus's love was not an erotic one. It's a fine line and is difficult to distinguish, in the experience of mystics; their love for Jesus is wholly passionate and involves their whole person. However, it's not an erotic love, strictly speaking; but rather, an agapic love which penetrates their erotic and fraternal love,[57] as Pope Benedict XVI explained so eloquently in his encyclical, *Deus Caritas Est*:

> Yet eros and agape—ascending love and descending love—can never be completely separated. The more the two, in their different aspects, find a proper unity

---

[57] *St. Thérèse of Lisieux by Those Who Knew Her: Testimonies from the Process of Beatification*, 247–48. (Testimony of Sr. Mary of the Trinity, recounting Thérèse's words and conduct regarding purity and modesty.)

in the one reality of love, the more the true nature of love in general is realized. Even if eros is at first mainly covetous and ascending, a fascination for the great promise of happiness, in drawing near to the other, it is less and less concerned with itself, increasingly seeks the happiness of the other, is concerned more and more with the beloved, bestows itself and wants to "be there for" the other. The element of agape thus enters into this love, for otherwise eros is impoverished and even loses its own nature. On the other hand, man cannot live by oblative, descending love alone. He cannot always give, he must also receive. Anyone who wishes to give love must also receive love as a gift. Certainly, as the Lord tells us, one can become a source from which rivers of living water flow (cf. Jn 7:37–38). Yet to become such a source, one must constantly drink anew from the original source, which is Jesus Christ, from whose pierced heart flows the love of God (cf. Jn 19:34).[58]

58 Pope Benedict XVI, *Deus Caritas Est: Encyclical Letter on*

Pope Benedict XVI states that, "In drawing near to the other, it is less and less concerned with itself, increasingly seeks the happiness of the other, is concerned more and more with the beloved, bestows itself and wants to 'be there for' the other." These words, it seems to me, perfectly describe Thérèse's spousal experience with her Beloved, Jesus.

6. Further developments of Thérèse's "spousal" relationship with Jesus

Let's move on now to another important episode in Thérèse's life which deeply influenced her spousal experience of Jesus: the day of her "complete conversion," as she defined it in the *Story of a Soul.* On Christmas Eve of 1886, when Thérèse was thirteen years old, she received a deep and lasting grace which we recounted in detail in the previous chapter. "Thérèse was no longer the same," she later wrote, "Jesus had changed her heart!" (cf. Ms A, 44v°–45v°). And she continued: "I felt *charity* enter into my soul, and the need to forget myself and to please others; since then

---

Christian Love, no. 7, December 25, 2005, accessed March 27, 2025, https://www.vatican.va/content/benedict-xvi/en/encyclicals/documents/hfben-xvienc20051225deus-caritas-est.html

I've been happy!" In the very next sentence, Thérèse starts to narrate her spiritual zeal for souls: "One Sunday, looking at a picture of Our Lord on the Cross [. . .], I was resolved to remain in spirit at the foot of the Cross and to receive the divine dew. I understood I was then to pour it out upon souls" (cf. Ms A, 45v°). It was then that she heard about a criminal Henri Pranzini, destined for the Guillotine. "I wanted at all costs to prevent him from falling into hell, and to attain my purpose I employed every means imaginable" (cf. Ms A, 45v°), Thérèse recounted. "He had mounted the scaffold and was preparing to place his head in the formidable opening, when suddenly, seized by an inspiration, he turned, took hold of the *crucifix* the priest was holding out to him and *kissed* the *sacred wounds three times!*" (Ms A, 46r°). The "lips of my '*first child*' *were* pressed to the sacred wounds!" (Ms A, 46v°), Thérèse concluded. She then turned to an even wider horizon, stating: "After this unique grace my desire to save souls grew each day" (Ms A, 46v°); and she continued, writing:

> It was a true interchange of love: to souls I was giving the *blood of Jesus*, to Jesus I was offering these same souls refreshed by the *divine dew*. I slaked His thirst and the

> more I gave Him *to drink*, the more the thirst of my poor little soul increased, and it was this ardent thirst He was giving me as the most delightful drink of His love.[59]

Just after telling of the "grace of leaving my childhood," as she defined it, Thérèse pressed on in her *Manuscript* A, recalling her "first child," Pranzini. This experience, for her, was not only that of a "spiritual maternity." This "first child," as well as many other souls, was "born" precisely out of the "true interchange of love" between Jesus and Thérèse. A spiritual, spousal love that generated spiritual children.

Thérèse, now freed from her childish way of being, started to grow: physically, emotionally, and spiritually. "I was at the most dangerous age for young girls," Thérèse stated in her *Manuscript* A. Then she continued, quoting the Prophet Ezekiel:

> But God did for me what Ezekiel reports in his prophecies: Passing by me, Jesus saw that the time had come for me to be *loved*, He entered into a covenant with me and I became *His own*. He spread

[59] *Story of a Soul*, trans. John Clarke, OCD, study ed. Marc Foley, OCD, "Autobiographical Manuscript dedicated to Mother Agnes of Jesus," 46.

> His mantle over me, He washed me with precious perfumes, He reclothed me in embroidered robes, He gave me priceless necklaces and ornaments. He nourished me with purest flour, with honey and oil in *abundance*. Then I became beautiful in His eyes and He made me a mighty queen.[60]

Thérèse quotes this rather crude and explicit passage of Ezekiel, which speaks of a baby girl who had been aborted and left to die in a field, but noted by the king, he takes her in and she later becomes his bride. Thérèse had no fear in applying to herself these explicit passages of scripture, especially the Song of Songs. She even remarked, toward the end of her life, that she would have gladly written a commentary on the Song of Songs, if she had had more time to do so. Thérèse most probably found this passage of Ezekiel while reading St. John of the Cross's *Spiritual Canticle*. In fact, St. John of the Cross was crucial for the growth and development of Thérèse's spousal love for Jesus.

---

[60] *Story of a Soul*, trans. John Clarke, OCD, study ed. Marc Foley, OCD, "Autobiographical Manuscript dedicated to Mother Agnes of Jesus," 47.

However, it's important to mention that even before Thérèse's entrance into Carmel, she saw her future life as a nun as a way of espousing and giving herself entirely to Jesus. On March 18, 1888, about three weeks before her entrance into Carmel, she wrote to Pauline (Sr. Agnes of Jesus): "Oh, Pauline, when Jesus will have placed me on the blessed shore of Carmel, I want to give myself totally to Him. I want to live no longer but for Him [. . .]. I desire only one thing when I shall be in Carmel, and it is to suffer always for Jesus."[61]

7. Thérèse's "spousal" relationship with Jesus in Carmel

As stated earlier, it was common knowledge and common usage among nuns in Thérèse's time to consider themselves as brides of Jesus. Even the public ceremonies reflected this. The Clothing Ceremony, or taking of the habit, was celebrated almost as if it were a wedding. The postulant, who on the Clothing Ceremony became a novitiate, exited from the monastery to greet her family and friends. Dressed in a wedding gown, the novitiate would be led to the altar by her father, just as in a wedding. She would assist the Mass, until the

---

61 *General Correspondence, Vol. I*, trans. John Clarke, OCD, 43.

homily, in her wedding dress. She would then go in procession to the chorus of the nuns, where she would be dressed with her new monastic habit. Thérèse narrates in her *Manuscript* A that she "had always wished that on the day I received the habit, nature would be adorned in white [snow] just like me." And she continued, describing the day of her Clothing Ceremony: "What thoughtfulness on the part of Jesus! Anticipating the desires of His fiancée, He gave her snow. Snow! What mortal bridegroom, no matter how powerful he may be, could make snow fall from heaven to charm his beloved?" (cf. Ms A, 72r°–72v°). Thérèse speaks of herself, here, as a "fiancée" and of Jesus as her "bridegroom." In fact, for Thérèse, her Clothing Ceremony—but most especially her Profession—were really and truly her "wedding day" with Jesus, her Spouse.

In the months following her father's illness and recovery in the hospital, Thérèse sought light and guidance. She asked her Novice Mistress, Sr. Mary of the Angels, who was also the librarian at the time, to be able to borrow some writings of St. John of the Cross. She was given a book which included both the *Spiritual Canticle* and the *Living Flame of Love*. Thérèse was able to keep the book with her because there were two copies of it in the Lisieux Carmel library. She read it and re-read it, and even kept it on her bedside table in the infirmary up until her death. "Ah! how many lights have I not drawn from the works of our holy father, St. John of the Cross! At the ages of seventeen and eighteen I had no other spiritual nourishment" (cf. Ms A, 83r°), she would later write in her *Manuscript* A. St. John of the Cross's powerful and symbolic language, so dense and full of love, intrigued Thérèse. "He is the saint of love *par excellence,*" she confided to Sr. Mary of the Trinity.[62] Thérèse, too, desired to live—and, I am convinced, effectively did live—a "spiritual matrimony" with Jesus, as St. John of the Cross praises and extols in his poems and spiritual treatises.

For Thérèse, as we said above, the day of her Profession was truly her wedding day with Jesus. It was tradition to write a note on one's Profession Day, and wear it over one's heart, while pronouncing one's vows. It was said that Jesus would answer all of His bride's requests on their wedding day. And so Thérèse composed her *Prayer* 2, *Profession Note*, and wore it on her heart. Not only on that day, though. She placed it into a pouch and wore it over her heart, together with some relics and other documents important to her, until the end of her days. In her *Profession Note*, she wrote:

---

[62] See "De nouveaux CSM [Conseils et Souvenirs de Marie de la Trinité] (nos. 31–57)," *Vie Thérésienne* 77 (1980): 62.

O Jesus, my divine spouse! May I never lose the second robe of my Baptism! Take me before I can commit the slightest voluntary fault. May I never seek nor find anything but yourself alone. May creatures be nothing for me and may I be nothing for them, but may you, Jesus, be *everything!* . . . May the things of earth never be able to trouble my soul, and may nothing disturb my peace. Jesus, I ask you for nothing but peace, and also love, infinite love without any limits other than yourself; love that is no longer I but you, my Jesus. Jesus, may I die a martyr for you. Give me martyrdom of heart or of body, or rather give me both . . . Give me the grace to fulfill my vows in all their perfection, and make me understand what a real spouse of yours should be. Never let me be a burden to the community, let nobody be occupied with me, let me be looked on as one to be trampled underfoot, forgotten like your little grain of sand, Jesus. May your will be done in me perfectly, and may I arrive at the place you have prepared for me. . . . Jesus, allow

> me to save very many souls; let no soul be damned today; let all the souls in purgatory be saved . . . Jesus, pardon me if I say anything I should not say. I want only to give you joy and to console you.

Thérèse refers to Jesus as her Spouse (époux), and to herself as His bride or spouse (épouse). The whole tone of the prayer is clearly spousal. There is no doubt of this. Thérèse expresses herself explicitly in her *Manuscript* A, when she recounts of her Reception of the Veil, which took place on September 24. It was a follow-up ceremony to the Profession and again considered as part of the "wedding" with Jesus. (The Profession was done in the Chapter Room, only with the celebrant and the other nuns. The Reception of the Veil was done in the church, with the presence of the family and friends of the nun.) During the same time period, her cousin Jeanne Guérin was preparing for her wedding with Dr. Francis La Néele. Thérèse wrote:

> Jeanne's wedding took place eight days after I received the veil. It would be impossible, dear Mother, for me to tell you how much I learned from her example concerning the delicate attentions a bride can bestow upon her bridegroom. I

listened eagerly to what she was saying so that I would learn all I could since I didn't want to do less for my beloved Jesus than Jeanne did for her Francis; true, he was a perfect creature, but he was still only a *creature!* I even went so far as to amuse myself to composing a letter of invitation [to my Reception of the Veil] which was comparable to Jeanne's own letter, and this is how it was written:

Letter of Invitation to the Wedding of Sister Thérèse of the Child Jesus and the Holy Face. God Almighty, Creator of Heaven and Earth, Sovereign Ruler of the Universe, and the Most Glorious Virgin Mary, Queen of the Heavenly Court, announce to you the Spiritual Espousals of Their August Son, Jesus, King of kings, and Lord of lords, with little Thérèse Martin, now Princess and Lady of His Kingdoms of the Holy Childhood and the Passion, assigned to her in dowry by her Divine Spouse, from which Kingdoms she holds her titles of nobility—of the Child Jesus and the Holy Face. Monsieur Louis Martin, Proprietor and

Master of the Domains of Suffering and Humiliation and Madame Martin, Princess and Lady of Honor of the Heavenly Court, wish to have you take part in the Marriage of their Daughter, Thérèse, with Jesus, the Word of God, the Second Person of the Adorable Trinity, Who through the operation of the Holy Spirit was made Man and Son of Mary, Queen of Heaven. Being unable to invite you to the Nuptial Blessing which was given on Mount Carmel, September 8, 1890, (the heavenly court alone was admitted), you are nevertheless asked to be present at the Return from the Wedding which will take place Tomorrow, the Day of Eternity, on which day Jesus, Son of God, will come on the Clouds of Heaven in the splendor of His Majesty, to judge the Living and the Dead. The hour being as yet uncertain, you are invited to hold yourselves in readiness and to watch.[63]

---

63 *Story of a Soul*, trans. John Clarke, OCD, study ed. Marc Foley, OCD, "Autobiographical Manuscript dedicated to Mother Marie de Gonzague."

8. Some conclusive thoughts

As Thérèse says, immediately after this long passage above: "What more is there to say?" I'll only hint to some final details regarding Thérèse's spousal experience with Jesus. I say "Jesus," and not "God," for a reason. Of course, her spousal experience—as St. John of the Cross teaches—immersed her in the life of the Trinity; however, Thérèse preferred to speak of Jesus, when speaking of her spousal experience. Actually, she usually referred even to God with the term "*Jésus.*" "*Jésus*" recurs for a total of 1,616 times in Thérèse's writings[64]; whereas, the term "God" ("*Dieu*") recurs for a total of 895 times. Scholars speak of her theology, in fact, as being a Trinitarian Christocentrism. The center, in other words, is Christ, but the whole Trinity is equally present.

In the last years of Thérèse's life, marked by her sickness and especially by her trial of faith, Thérèse's devotion to the Holy Face grew, and her spousal experience with Jesus was greatly influenced by her

---

[64] See the Concordances of Thérèse's writings: *Les mots de Sainte Thérèse de l'Enfant-Jésus et de la Sainte-Face: Concordance générale*, ed. Sœur Geneviève, O.P., de Clairefontaine, Sœur Cécile, O.C.D., du Carmel de Lisieux, and Jacques Lonchampt (Lonrai, Orne: Les Éditions du Cerf, 1996), 465.

devotion to Christ's Passion. Think of, for example, her *Prayer* 12, *Consecration to the Holy Face*, which is a prayer with clear spousal tonalities. At the same time, her spousal experience was not entirely focused on the Holy Face. I would say that it was more ample than that. It contemplates Jesus in the entirety of His Mystery and His Person. Thérèse loves Jesus, the God-Man. A glance at a couple of her poems will suffice. In her *Poem* 36, "Jesus alone"—in the midst of her trial of faith—Thérèse wrote (on August 15, 1896):

> It's to you alone, Jesus, that I'm attached.
>
> It's into your arms that I run and hide.
> I want to love you like a little child.
> I want to fight like a brave warrior.
> Like a child full of little attentions,
> Lord, I want to overwhelm you with caresses,
>
> And in the field of my apostolate,
> Like a warrior I throw myself into the fight!.

In Thérèse's *Poem* 41, "How I Want to Love," instead, she wrote (toward the end of 1896):

> Divine Jesus, listen to my prayer.

By my love I want to make you rejoice.
You know well, I want to please you alone.
Deign to grant my most ardent desire.
I accept the trials of this sad exile
To delight you and to console your heart.
But change all my works into love,
O my Spouse, my Beloved Savior.

Thérèse's spousal experience with Jesus accompanied her, of course, until the very end. On September 25, 1897, only five days before her holy death, someone remarked: "Ah! it's frightful what you're suffering." And Thérèse responded: "No, it is not frightful. A little victim of love cannot find frightful what her Spouse sends her through love."[65] Thérèse, in the last years of her life, had often written and spoken about her desire of "dying of love." She had discovered this desire through St. John of the Cross. She was well-prepared for a "death of love," which she had so ardently desired. And so it was: grasping tightly to her Crucifix—the one she had touched to many relics in Rome, and which she loved to often

[65] St. Thérèse of Lisieux, *Yellow Notebook*, 9.25.3 (September 25, 1897).

kiss[66]—Thérèse gazed upon it in her final moments and pronounced clearly her last words: "Oh! I love Him! . . . My God, I love you!"[67]

---

66 St. Thérèse of Lisieux, *General Correspondence*, vol. 2: *1890–1897*, trans. John Clarke, O.C.D. (Washington, DC: ICS Publications, 2014), 1173–74 (Letter 263, to Fr. Bellière, August 10, 1897).

67 St. Thérèse of Lisieux, *Yellow Notebook*, September 30, 1897.

From left to right: St. Zélie Guérin (Thérèse's mother). Rose Taillé (Thérèse's wet nurse), © Archives du Carmel de Lisieux. Used with permission. Thérèse's elder sister Pauline Martin.

On the left: Thérèse's eldest sister, Marie Martin (at 21 years of age).

On the right: the statue of "The Virgin of the Smile." Photo Frédéric Moreau © Archives du Carmel de Lisieux. Used with permission.

CHAPTER FOUR

The Blessed Virgin Mary and Spiritual Maternity in Thérèse

1. Introduction: the meaning of loss and suffering in Thérèse

In this chapter dedicated to Thérèse's relationship with the Blessed Virgin Mary and her own experience of "spiritual maternity," we'll witness a story of grace. Thérèse received various profound wounds and sufferings in her life. I would say that she received at least four very profound "wounds," in her brief time on earth, to not mention the smaller ones: 1) at four years of age, the loss of her mother, with all its psychological consequences; 2) from ages fifteen to twenty-one, the illness and subsequent death of her father; 3) at twenty-three years of age, her trial of faith (for the rest of her life); 4) and, contemporarily, her sickness and death at age twenty-four.

In the previous chapter, we saw how the meditation of the Passion of Christ, especially seen through and in His Holy Face, gave strength and meaning to the sufferings due to the illness and death of her father. In this chapter, we'll be analyzing the death of her mother Zélie and how she coped with it, finding in Mary a new and special maternity; in our final chapter, we'll study the "Passion" and "Death of love" of Thérèse, taking a closer look, then, at her spiritual and physical sufferings due to her trial of faith and her sickness.

These facts will lead us to discover one of the most fascinating and very relevant aspects of Thérèse's experience for modern-day man. It is quite precisely in the suffering and in the fragility (even psychological) of Thérèse that we can find a reason for hope. We'll see how Thérèse's "strength" resides in her positive attitude and reaction to her many sufferings; however, it's not simply a question of having a positive attitude: it's a question of her complete trust and abandonment in God, in which the secret of her strength, resilience, or rather *genius*, resides. It's possible even for those who have suffered greatly to discover God's tenderness and His overwhelming and transforming love. Afterall, Thérèse did so . . . why not us, as well? As Thérèse affirmed in her *Story of a Soul*:

> Yes, suffering opened wide its arms to me and I threw myself into them with love. I had declared at the feet of Jesus-Victim, in the examination preceding my profession, what I had come to Carmel for: "I came to save souls and especially to pray for priests." When one wishes to attain a goal, one must use the means; Jesus made me understand that it was through suffering that He wanted to give me souls, and my attraction for suffering grew in proportion to its increase. This was my way for five years; exteriorly nothing revealed my suffering, which was all the more painful since I alone was aware of it. Ah! what a surprise we shall have at the end of the world when we shall read the story of souls! There will be those who will be surprised when they see the way through which my soul was guided![68]

Thérèse made a choice, in her life: she had already suffered "passively," as it were, with the death of her

---

68 *Story of a Soul*, trans. John Clarke, OCD, study ed. Marc Foley, OCD, "Autobiographical Manuscript dedicated to Mother Marie de Gonzague," 69–70.

mother and all its aftermath, which we'll be examining shortly. She made a choice: "When one wishes to attain a goal," she wrote, "one must use the means; Jesus made me understand that it was through suffering that He wanted to give me souls, and my attraction for suffering grew in proportion to its increase." Thérèse "utilized" suffering—inevitable in this life—as a "means," an "instrument," to attain her goal: the salvation of souls. And, for her, that suffering was a pledge, a token, of eternal glory. In her *Prayer 6*, *Act of Oblation to Merciful Love*, she wrote:

> I thank you, O my God! for all the graces You have granted me, especially the grace of making me pass through the crucible of suffering. It is with joy I shall contemplate You on the last day carrying the scepter of Your Cross. Since You deigned to give me a share in this very precious Cross, I hope in Heaven to resemble You and to see shining in my glorified body the sacred stigmata of Your Passion. . . .

Thérèse did not receive the mystical phenomenon of the stigmata during her earthly life. Yet, "I hope in Heaven to resemble You," she wrote, "and to see shining in my glorified body the sacred stigmata of Your

Passion." For Thérèse, the wounds received in life—the death of her mother, the sickness and death of her father, her own sickness and death, and her trial of faith—were a pledge of eternal glory: "I hope [. . .] to see shining in my glorified body the sacred stigmata of Your Passion." God transfigured Thérèse's wounds, even during her earthly life: in the midst of humiliations and suffering, the Holy Spirit moved Thérèse to transform and transfigure all into love. And love is eternal. Our wounds *can and will* be transfigured one day.

2. The loss(es) of her mother(s)

Let's take a closer look now at one of the deepest wounds that Thérèse received, the loss of her mother, and how the Blessed Virgin Mary came to her aid, rendering Thérèse, in turn, a spiritual mother for many. This is the paradoxical and wonderful reality that Thérèse experienced: a motherless girl who becomes a spiritual mother for thousands, or rather millions of people. The source of such fruitfulness, of course, can only come from God, as the Letter to the Ephesians says: "For this reason I kneel before the Father, from whom every paternity in heaven and on earth derives its name" (Eph. 3:14–15). God participated something of His paternity and fruitfulness to Thérèse, as did the Blessed Virgin Mary, of her maternity.[69]

To begin with, it's important to remember that Thérèse suffered, even before her mother's death, a kind of "maternal mourning."[70] Newborn Thérèse refused her mother's breast, I would say instinctively:

---

69 M. E. Patrizi, *Il Patto segreto: L'amicizia mistica di san Massimiliano Kolbe e santa Teresa di Lisieux* (Rome: C.d.C. Editrice, 2008). (Considering that Kolbe's spirituality is largely based on the dogma of the Immaculate Conception, Thérèse's relationship with Mary is also addressed in this study.) See also: M. E. Patrizi, "P. Kolbe e la spiritualità di Santa Teresa di Gesù Bambino," *Rivista di Vita Spirituale* 53 (1999): 188–209. For further insights regarding Thérèse's relationship with Mary and her vocation to be "love in the heart of the Church," see: M. E. Patrizi, "'La mia vocazione è l'amore'. Sulla scia di Maria," *Rivista di Vita Spirituale* 6 (1997): 753–62; M. E. Patrizi, "S. Teresa di Lisieux: 'Nella Chiesa io sarò l'amore'," *La Madonna delle Laste* 11 (1996): 11.

70 A. Assailly, "Thérèse, sœur des hommes dans les épreuves," *Annales de Sainte Thérèse de Lisieux* 2 (1973): 7–12; L. Gayral, "Une maladie nerveuse dans l'enfance de Sainte Thérèse de Lisieux," *Carmel* (1959): 81–96. See also: Luis Jorge González, *Teresa di Lisieux. Intelligenza emotiva e Counseling spirituale* (Rome: Edizioni OCD, 2019); J. Maître, *L'Orpheline de la Béresina. Thérèse de Lisieux (1873–1897)* (Paris: Cerf, 1996), 194–202

Zélie had breast cancer, in fact, and was unable to breastfeed her babies. Zélie remarked about this fact to her brother, Isidore, in her letter on March 1, 1873: "[Thérèse] is very sick and I have no hope of saving her"; and, she concluded the letter, "I often think of the mothers who have the joy of feeding, themselves, their babies; and I, I must see them all die one after the other!"[71] Her doctor, however, insisted that she find a wet nurse for Thérèse. Zélie went to call for Rose Taillé. After a feeding, little Thérèse fell asleep and then awoke with a smile on her face.[72] The only hope was to entrust her to the wet nurse; and thus began Thérèse's first "mourning," so to speak: for more than a year, Thérèse had to live in the wet nurse's household, a good eight kilometers from Alençon and her family.[73] Father Luis Jorge Gonzalez writes: "Having been

---

71 Carmel of Lisieux Archives, "Letter of Zélie Martin to her brother Isidore Guérin, March 1, 1872," LC [Letters between (Thérèse's) Correspondents], no. 87, accessed March 27, 2025, https://archives.carmeldelisieux.fr/en/correspondance/de-mme-martin-a-son-frere-isidore-guerin-cf-87-1er-mars-1873/.

72 Guy Gaucher, *Saint Thérèse of Lisieux: The Story of a Life* (San Francisco: Ignatius Press, 2020), 21–22.

73 *Sainte Thérèse de l'Enfant-Jésus et de la Sainte-Face: Œuvres complètes (Textes et Dernières Paroles)* (Lonrai: Éditions du Cerf/Desclée De Brouwer, 1992), 1479. (Thérèse was

torn from her mother's arms [. . .], [Thérèse] runs the risk of experiencing the 'hospitalism syndrome.' This pathological case [can develop] in the child who, having experienced the emotional bond of maternal love, feels deprived of it suddenly and abruptly."[74] Of course, visits from her parents and sisters were frequent; but Thérèse became accustomed to Rose's maternal presence. Gonzalez comments: "On the one hand, Thérèse's positive relationship with Rose allows her to develop that basic trust that, according to Erikson, is installed in the human being during the first year of life. On the other hand, precisely because the affective bond becomes tight, its rupture can only be traumatic." Gonzalez thus speaks of a "double trauma": the temporary "loss" of her mother Zélie, and the "loss," again, of the nanny Rose Taillé, once she had fulfilled her duty.[75] Regarding these early, quite traumatic months of Thérèse's existence, Dr. Gayral points out:

---

brought to Semallé, to the wet nurse's home, on March 16, 1873; she returned definitively to Alençon on April 2, 1874.)

[74] Luis Jorge González, *Teresa di Lisieux. Intelligenza emotiva e Counseling spirituale*, 53. (Translation mine.)

[75] Luis Jorge González, *Teresa di Lisieux. Intelligenza emotiva e Counseling spirituale*, 54.

> It is extremely important to note that the first months of Thérèse's life were marked by severe digestive disorders that endangered her life because, rightly so, it is not uncommon for these incidents to have late repercussions, not only on physical development but especially – though this is less obvious – on one's character [or personality]. The first relations with the world are made in the oral mode, and when [these relations] are disturbed and unsatisfactory, it frequently happens that the whole being receives the mark. These children are more sensitive and subsequently tolerate affective frustrations less than others.[76]

Let's jump ahead in time, to Zélie's death: I'm sure you remember the tender episode we evoked in our first chapter, which Zélie recounted in a letter to her daughter Pauline: "When [Thérèse] saw herself so well received, she said to me, 'Oh! Mama, if only you were to wrap me in a blanket like when I was little! I'd

---

[76] L. Gayral, "Une maladie nerveuse dans l'enfance de Sainte Thérèse de Lisieux," *Carmel* (1959): 89. (Translation mine.)

eat my chocolate here at the table.' I took the trouble to go look for her blanket and then I wrapped her in it like when she was little. I looked like I was playing with a doll!"[77] Moments like these, so tender and beautiful, must certainly have edified the developing personality of little Thérèse. However, the little girl was not adequately prepared for her mother's impending death, let alone guarded in the dramatic moments around her passing. I think it is sufficient, in this regard, to listen to Thérèse, who, now twenty-two years old, evokes the sad memories of that moment, in her Manuscript A:

> The touching ceremony of the last anointing is also deeply impressed on my mind. I can still see the spot where I was by Céline's side. All five of us were lined up according to age, and Papa was there too, sobbing. The day of Mama's departure or the day after, Papa took me in his arms and said: "Come, kiss your poor little mother for the last time." Without a word I placed my lips on her forehead. I don't

[77] Carmel of Lisieux Archives, "Letter of Zélie Guérin Martin to Pauline, February 13, 1877," accessed March 27, 2025, https://archives.carmeldelisieux.fr/en/correspondance/de-mme-martin-a-pauline-cf-188-13-fevrier-1877/.

> recall having cried very much, neither did I speak to anyone about the feelings I experienced. I looked and listened in silence. No one had any time to pay any attention to me, and I saw many things they would have hidden from me. For instance, once I was standing before the lid of the coffin which had been placed upright in the hall. I stopped for a long time gazing at it. Though I'd never seen one before, I understood what it was. I was so little that in spite of Mama's small stature, I had to raise my head to take in its full height. It appeared *large* and *dismal*.[78]

We are facing a very important grief: that of a four-year-old girl losing her beloved mother. There is no need, I think, to expand on this point. Gonzalez comments, in this regard, "We are faced with an irrefutable fact: Thérèse's human development came to a halt with the death of her mother."[79]

---

[78] *Story of a Soul*, trans. John Clarke, OCD, study ed. Marc Foley, OCD, "Autobiographical Manuscript dedicated to Mother Marie de Gonzague," 12.

[79] González, *Teresa di Lisieux. Intelligenza emotiva e Counseling spirituale*, 56. (Translation from Italian to English is my own.)

I would like to underline two aspects of this very traumatic period in Thérèse's life. On the one hand, her character changes completely. She herself stated this; in her *Manuscript* A, she wrote:

> I must admit, Mother, my happy disposition completely changed after Mama's death. I, once so full of life, became timid and retiring, sensitive to an excessive degree. One look was enough to reduce me to tears, and the only way I was content was to be left alone completely. I could not bear the company of strangers and found my joy only within the intimacy of the family.

Thérèse withdraws, therefore, into herself, perhaps out of an instinct of self- defense and self-preservation. Another defense mechanism comes naturally to the child: on the very day of Zélie's funeral, Céline threw herself into the arms of Marie, her older sister, saying, "Well! you will be my Mama." Thérèse imitates Céline, but turns to Pauline, the second-born, exclaiming, "Well! as for me, it's Pauline who will be my Mama!"

3. Another maternal loss, a "strange sickness," a sudden healing

Let's jump forward in time to Thérèse's ninth year of age. She had already lost her mother Zélie and had chosen Pauline as her "second mother." Now the Lord was permitting yet another loss to open the way to another "gain": another Mother. Once again, Thérèse undergoes a sudden detachment from her motherly figure. This time it is her "second mother," Pauline. But let us listen to Thérèse herself recount this moment:

> I had said to Pauline, one day, that I would like to be a hermit and go away with her alone in a faraway desert place. She answered that my desire was also hers and that she *was waiting* for me to be big enough for her to leave. This was no doubt not said seriously, but little Thérèse had taken it seriously; and how she suffered when she heard her dear Pauline speaking one day to Marie about her coming entrance into Carmel. I didn't know what Carmel was, but I understood that Pauline was going to leave me to enter a convent. I understood, too, she *would not wait for me* and I was about

> to lose my second *mother!* Ah! how can I express the anguish of my heart! In one instant, I understood what life was; until then, I had never seen it so sad; but it appeared to me in all its reality, and I saw it was nothing but a continual suffering and separation. I shed bitter tears because I did not yet understand the *joy* of sacrifice. I was *weak*, so *weak* that I consider it a great grace to have been able to support a trial that seemed to be far above my strength! If I had learned of my dear Pauline's departure very gently, I would not have suffered as much perhaps, but having heard about it by surprise, it was as if a sword were buried in my heart.[80]

Such a sudden and painful separation from her "second mother," Pauline, was perhaps bearable for Thérèse's strong and spiritual soul, but certainly unbearable for her still fragile psyche. Thérèse therefore fell ill, of what she would call "*une si étrange maladie*" ("strange illness") (cf. Ms A, 28v°). Now, there is no time to make

---

[80] *Story of a Soul*, trans. John Clarke, OCD, study ed. Marc Foley, OCD, "Autobiographical Manuscript dedicated to Mother Marie de Gonzague," 25.

a minute examination of this illness, which lasted from the end of March until May 13, 1883.[81]

However, I would like to recall just one detail, I would call fundamental: I will let Thérèse herself tell it:

> One evening Uncle took me for a walk and spoke about Mama and about past memories with a kindness that touched me profoundly and made me cry. Then he told me I was too softhearted, that I needed a lot of distraction, and he was determined to give us a good time during our Easter vacation. He and Aunt would see to it. That night we were to go to the Catholic Circle meeting, but finding I was too fatigued, Aunt made me go to bed; when I was undressing, I was seized with a strange trembling. Believing I was cold, Aunt covered me with blankets and surrounded me with hot water bottles. But nothing was able to stop my shaking, which lasted almost all night. Uncle, returning from the meeting with my

---

81 *Sainte Thérèse de l'Enfant-Jésus et de la Sainte-Face: Œuvres complètes* (Lonrai: Éditions du Cerf/Desclée De Brouwer, 1992), 1483.

> cousins and Céline, was very much surprised to see me in this state, which he judged to be very serious. He didn't want to say this in order not to frighten Aunt.

This is precisely how Thérèse's "strange illness" began: in a context closely related to the loss of her mother. In that month and a half, Thérèse will seek the protection and comfort, once again, of a motherly figure: her eldest sister, Marie. (Note that this would already be her fourth "motherly figure," after Zélie, her wet nurse Rose, and then Pauline.) Thérèse, recounting the period of her illness in her *Manuscript* A, would speak of Marie as having a "Mother's heart," and how her sister Marie, precisely, cared for and consoled her with the "tenderness of a Mother" (cf. Ms A, 28r°.29r°). Thérèse would not allow Marie to leave her, and would constantly call for her, saying "Mama! Mama!" until she returned to her bedside. So let us listen to Marie, her eldest sister, who later shared her memories in the year 1910, at the Process for Thérèse's beatification:

> Around the age of ten, the Servant of God was struck by a strange illness [. . .]. She had terrifying visions that chilled all who heard her cries of anguish. Certain nails, attached to the walls of the room,

would suddenly appear to her in the form of large charred fingers, and she would exclaim, "I'm afraid, I'm afraid!" Her eyes, so calm and gentle, had an expression of horror impossible to describe. Another time, my father came and sat beside her bed; he was holding his hat in his hand. Thérèse looked at him without saying a word, for she spoke little during this illness. Then, as always, in the blink of an eye, her expression changed. Her eyes stared at the hat and she let out a mournful cry, "Oh! the great black beast!" Her cries had something supernatural about them; one would have to have heard them to get an idea [. . .]. I can say that the devil even tried to kill our little sister. Her bed was arranged in a large alcove, and at her head and feet there was an empty space where she tried to throw herself into. It actually happened to her several times, and I wonder how she didn't smash her head on the floor; but she didn't even have a scratch. Other times she would bang her head, violently, against the wooden bedside. A few more times she wanted to

> speak to me but no sound could be heard. But the most terrible crisis of all was the one that [Thérèse] recounts in her "Life." I thought she was going to succumb. Seeing her exhausted in this painful struggle, I wanted to give her a drink, but she cried out in terror, "They want to poison me." It was then that I threw myself with my sisters at the feet of the Blessed Virgin. Three times I repeated the same prayer. The third time, I saw Thérèse staring at the statue of the Blessed Virgin. Her gaze was radiant and as if in ecstasy. She confided to me, [later], that she had seen the Blessed Virgin herself. This vision lasted four to five minutes, then her gaze fixed itself on me with tenderness. From that moment she seemed to have no trace of her illness.[82]

In a few lines, Mary Martin (Sr. Marie of the Sacred Heart) gives us a very precise and vivid description

---

[82] Carmel of Lisieux Archives, "Les témoignages du procès ordinaire – Témoin 3: Marie du Sacré-Cœur," accessed March 27, 2025, https://archives.carmeldelisieux.fr/en/naissance-dune-sainte/les-proces-la-sainte-de-therese/le-proces-ordinaire/les-temoignages-du-proces-ordinaire/#temoin-3-marie-du-sacre-coeur. (Translation mine.)

of Thérèse's serious illness, and also of the "smile of the Virgin," which lasted even four to five minutes! Thérèse would later write in her *Manuscript* A:

> All of a sudden the Blessed Virgin appeared *beautiful* to me, so *beautiful* that never had I seen anything so attractive; her face was suffused with an ineffable benevolence and tenderness, but what penetrated to the very depths of my soul was the "*ravishing smile of the Blessed Virgin.*" At that instant, all my pain disappeared, and two large tears glistened on my eyelashes, and flowed down my cheeks silently, but they were tears of unmixed joy.

4. Thérèse and the Blessed Virgin Mary

And so we've come to the "key" point of this Chapter . . . but in fact we must already turn, slowly, toward its conclusion: What, then, was Thérèse's relationship with Mary?

It must be said that her filial relationship toward the Blessed Virgin Mary does not begin here, with the experience of her "enchanting smile," but as early as five or six years old, for example—Thérèse recounts in her

Manuscript A: "Since I was too little to attend May devotions, I remained at home with Victoire, carrying out my devotions with her before *my little May altar*" (Ms A, 15v°). Or, toward the end of her sixth year or the beginning of her seventh year of age, Thérèse made her first confession. She wrote, "I remember the first exhortation directed to me. Father encouraged me to be devout to the Blessed Virgin and I promised myself to redouble my tenderness for her. Coming out of the confessional I was so happy and light-hearted that I had never felt so much joy in my soul" (cf. Ms A, 16v°–17r°).

Again, Thérèse's filial relationship with Mary does not begin with seeing Mary's "ravishing smile." Certainly, however, it was a fundamental moment. I dare say that, in that instant, Thérèse truly experienced her as a mother. In that moment there was, in fact, something like an overlapping of various "mothers." Shortly after her birth, in danger of death, she had been entrusted to a wet nurse, Rose Taillé, with whom she formed, in that year's-time, daughter-mother bonds; losing her mother Zélie at the age of four, Thérèse had taken Pauline as her "second mother." Upon Pauline's entrance to Carmel, she had taken her eldest sister Marie as her "third" (or rather, her "fourth") mother. And, on that Pentecost Sunday, May 13, 1883, Thérèse kept calling out for Marie, "Mama! . . . Mama!" But, in vain. No one could replace her mother, Zélie; no one could replace her "second mother," Pauline. No one could replace her "third mother," Marie, so much so that Léonie suffered because she understood—when she came to replace Marie for a little while—that Thérèse was not happy about it. (cf. Ms A, 29r°). But, again, no motherly figure was able to fill that void, that unprocessed and unhealed bereavement stemming from the loss of her mother Zélie. No earthly mother could help her anymore. No earthly mother was sufficient. And it was precisely then that our heavenly Mother, the Blessed Virgin Mary, intervened. "Finding no help on earth," Thérèse would later write, "poor little Thérèse had also turned toward the mother of heaven, and prayed with all her heart that she take pity on her. All of a sudden the Blessed Virgin appeared *beautiful* to me, so *beautiful* that never had I seen anything so attractive."

It is from this moment, I would say, that Thérèse experiences the powerful and sweet motherhood of Mary. And she will experience it more and more. A year later, on the day of her First Communion, Thérèse again experienced Mary's maternity in a powerful way. But also that of her mother Zélie. She wrote: "Oh! no, the absence of Mama didn't cause me any sorrow on the day of my First Communion. Wasn't Heaven itself in my soul, and hadn't Mama taken her place there a long time ago? Thus in receiving Jesus's visit, I received also Mama's. She blessed me and rejoiced at my happiness." And, regarding Mary's motherhood, she wrote:

> In the afternoon, it was I who made the Act of Consecration to the Blessed Virgin. It was only right that I *speak* in the name of my companions to my mother in heaven, I who had been deprived at such an early age of my earthly mother. I put all my heart into *speaking* to her, into consecrating myself to her as a child throwing itself into the arms of its mother, asking her to watch over her. It seems to me the Blessed Virgin must have looked upon her little flower and *smiled* at her, for wasn't it she who cured her with a *visible smile*? Had she not placed in the heart of her little flower her Jesus, the Flower of the Fields and the Lily of the valley?[83]

[83] *Story of a Soul*, trans. John Clarke, OCD, study ed. Marc Foley, OCD, "Autobiographical Manuscript dedicated to Mother Marie de Gonzague," 35.

I could continue this analysis of Thérèse's relationship with Our Lady, but unfortunately, there is no more time or space for it now. Thérèse would later rejoice and underline the fact that she made her Profession on September 8, 1890, the Feast of the Nativity of Mary. She would later entrust her autobiography to the Virgin, kneeling down in front of the same statue of Our Lady of Victories, now placed in the antechamber of her cell: "Before taking up my pen, I knelt before the statue of Mary [. . .] and I begged her to guide my hand that it trace no line displeasing to her" (cf. Ms A, 2r°). She dedicated her last Poem precisely to Mary: "I still have something to do before I die," she confided to Sr. Geneviéve (Céline); "I have always dreamed of expressing in a hymn to the Blessed Virgin all that I think of her" [84] . . . "You who came *to smile at me* in the morning of my life,/ Come smile at me again . . . Mother . . . It's evening now!" So she writes in the last stanza of her *Poem* 54, "Why I Love You, O Mary!" And even the last lines that Thérèse will trace on earth—with a trembling hand—she dedicates them to the Blessed Virgin: "O Mary, if I were Queen

---

[84] *Sainte Thérèse de l'Enfant-Jésus et de la Sainte-Face, Nouvelle Édition du Centenaire: Édition critique des Œuvres Complètes*, Poésies. (Lonrai: Éditions du Cerf/Desclée De Brouwer, 1992), 238. (Translation mine.)

of Heaven and you were Thérèse, I would want to be Thérèse so that you might be Queen of Heaven!!!" (Pr 21).[85] This was on September 8, 1897, the seventh anniversary of her Profession.[86]

[85] *Sainte Thérèse de l'Enfant-Jésus et de la Sainte-Face, Nouvelle Édition du Centenaire: Édition critique des Œuvres Complètes*, Récréations pieuses-Prières, 529 (55).
[86] *Sainte Thérèse de l'Enfant-Jésus et de la Sainte-Face*, Récréations pieuses-Prières, 621 (147).

The community of the Lisieux Carmel in April of 1895.

Céline Martin (Sr. Geneviève of the Holy Face) is on the bottom left of the picture; Sr. Mary of the Trinity (one of Thérèse's novices) is on Céline's right; to her right, Sr. Mary of the Sacred Heart (Marie Martin). Above Céline is Pauline Martin (Sr. Agnes of Jesus); to her right is Thérèse. On the right of Thérèse is Sr. Mary of the Angels, Thérèse's ex-novice mistress (who was also the Librarian who lent her St. John of the Cross's writings). Above Pauline, slightly toward the right, is the Prioress, Mother Marie de Gonzague.

CHAPTER FIVE

Fraternal Charity in Thérèse

1. Introduction: Fraternal charity in Thérèse: a multi-faceted experience

This study is a sort of "booklet" on Thérèse. It is therefore very condensed. Each chapter—and other topics besides—could easily be developed into a full book. (In fact, I'm teaching a full semester-long course at the "*Teresianum*" (Carmelite University in Rome) on "Fraternal Charity in St. Thérèse of Lisieux".) So, there is too much information on this topic to pack into just one chapter; that said, I'll do my best to offer you a balanced synthesis of Thérèse's experience of fraternal charity.

In my course on Thérèse's fraternal charity, I preferred to examine the question from various points of view. One might spontaneously think of her charity toward her nun-sisters in the monastery; and that is an extremely important aspect of her fraternal charity. Yet, that's not all. We've been analyzing the whole of Thérèse's experience, again, from various points of view. The same must be said of her fraternal charity, which is something like a multi-faceted "diamond." To be systematic and try to acquire an overall view of Thérèse's fraternal charity, one must examine her charity toward various categories of persons whom she met and lived with during the course of her lifetime. One must consider, thus, Thérèse's charity toward her family members; toward sinners; toward priests; toward her nun-sisters; toward her spiritual sons and daughters; but even toward holy souls in Purgatory and in Heaven; and, lastly, toward all men and women of all time. Her *régard*—her vision, her perspective—and her charity embrace all three states of the Church: militant, purgative, and triumphant. Yes, Thérèse's fraternal charity is truly universal, and crosses all borders (even of time) to embrace all men and all women of all time. She participated, in a special way, in God's infinite and universal charity. Let's take a closer look.

2. Fraternal charity in the Martin family

As I mentioned in our chapter on Thérèse's spousal experience, Thérèse received an extraordinary example of fraternal charity from her parents, Saints Louis and Zélie Martin. We must remember that spousal love also includes a fraternal type of love, as the lovers in the Biblical book, the Song of Songs remind us: "You have stolen my heart, my sister, my bride; you have stolen my heart with one glance of your eyes, with one jewel of your necklace. How delightful is your love, my sister, my bride! How much more pleasing is your love than wine, and the fragrance of your perfume more than any spice!" (Song 4:9–10). Most certainly Louis and Zélie Martin loved each other, as well, with a strong and unbreakable tie of fraternal charity.

Thérèse grew up, then, in a family atmosphere permeated by fraternal charity. Thérèse testifies to this in the first pages of her *Manuscript* A:

> God was pleased all through my life to surround me with *love*, and the first memories I have are stamped with smiles and the most tender caresses. But although He placed so much *love* near me, He also sent much love into my little heart, making it warm and affectionate. I loved Mama and Papa very much and showed my tenderness for them in a thousand ways, for I was very expressive.

Thérèse states that her "first memories" were "stamped with smiles and the most tender caresses." Most certainly she did not receive them only from her parents, but also from her four sisters, Marie, Pauline, Léonie, and Céline. In the first pages of her childhood memoirs—later called *Manuscript* A—Thérèse writes about each of her siblings. She wrote:

> I was very fond of my *godmother* [Marie]. Without appearing to do so, I paid close attention to what was said and done around me. It seems to me that I was judging things then as I do now. I was listening carefully to what Marie was teaching Céline in order to do what Céline did.

Thérèse thus finds in Marie and in Céline a role model, an example; but she also mentions Léonie, stating:

> Dear little Léonie held a warm place in my heart. She was very fond of me and in the evenings when the family took a walk she used to take care of me. I still seem to hear those beautiful lullabies she used to sing to me to get me to sleep. She was always trying to find ways of pleasing me,

> and I would be sorry if I caused her any trouble.[87]

Léonie was very dear to Thérèse; but since the beginning, another of her sisters had held a special place in her heart. Thérèse wrote, again in the first pages of her *Manuscript* A: "I was very proud of my two sisters [Marie and Céline], but the one who was my *ideal* from childhood was Pauline. When I was beginning to talk, Mama would ask me: 'What are you thinking about?' and I would answer invariably: 'Pauline!'" This is why Thérèse chose, on the day of her mother's funeral, Pauline as her second mother. Her attachment to Pauline, even as an infant, proved to be providential in God's plan for Thérèse. She wrote, in the next lines of her *Manuscript* A:

> I had often heard it said that surely Pauline would become a *religious*, and without knowing too much about what it meant I thought: "I too *will be a religious*". This is one of my first memories and I haven't changed my resolution since then! It was through you, dear Mother,

[87] *Story of a Soul*, trans. John Clarke, OCD, study ed. Marc Foley, OCD, "Autobiographical Manuscript dedicated to Mother Marie de Gonzague," 4-6.

> that Jesus chose to espouse me to Himself [. . .]. You were my *ideal*; I wanted to be like you, and it was your example that drew me toward the Spouse of Virgins at the age of two.

3. The beginnings of Thérèse's fraternal charity toward the nuns in the Lisieux Carmel

Speaking of Thérèse's vocation to "be a religious," felt from the age of two, let's jump forward to Thérèse's ties of fraternal charity with her nun-sisters. (That is, with her future nun-sisters.) After Thérèse had suddenly and unexpectedly learned of Pauline's nearing departure for Carmel, she reflected on these events and clarified even her own vocation. She would later write in her *Manuscript* A, addressed of course to her own sister Pauline, now Mother Agnes of Jesus:

> I shall always remember, dear Mother, with what tenderness you consoled me. Then you explained the life of Carmel to me and it seemed so beautiful! When thinking over all you had said, I felt that Carmel was the *desert* where God wanted me to go also to hide myself. I felt this with so much force that there wasn't the

> least doubt in my heart; it was not the dream of a child led astray but the *certitude* of a divine call; I wanted to go to Carmel not for *Pauline's sake* but for *Jesus alone*. I was thinking *very much* about things that words could not express but which left a great peace in my soul.[88]

The next day, Thérèse confided her secret to Pauline. She wrote: "[Pauline] considered my desires as the will of heaven and told me that soon I would go with her to see the Mother Prioress of the Carmel and that I must tell her what God was making me feel. A Sunday was chosen for this solemn visit [. . .]" (Ms A, 26r°). This visit took place during the summer of 1882, when Thérèse was nine years old. Shortly after Pauline's entrance, on October 2, 1882, Thérèse went again to the Carmel parlor to visit her sister, now Sr. Agnes of Jesus, and saw the Prioress Mother Marie de Gonzague for the second time. A month or two later, Thérèse wrote a letter to the Prioress, her *Letter* 9. She wrote:

---

[88] *Story of a Soul*, trans. John Clarke, OCD, study ed. Marc Foley, OCD, "Autobiographical Manuscript dedicated to Mother Marie de Gonzague," 26.

Dear Mother,

It has been a long time since I saw you, so I am very happy to write you to tell you about my little affairs. Pauline told me you were on retreat, and I'm coming to ask you to pray to little Jesus for me because I have many faults and want to correct them.

I have to make my confession to you. For some time, I am always answering Marie back when she tells me to do something. It seems when Pauline was little and when she made excuses to Aunt at Le Mans, Aunt used to say to her: So many holes, so many pegs! But with me it's even worse. So I want to correct myself, and, into each little hole, put a pretty little flower which I'll offer to little Jesus to prepare myself for my First Communion. Won't you, dear Mother, pray for this? Oh! yes, this beautiful moment will come quickly, and how happy I shall be to have so many flowers to offer Him when the little Jesus comes into my heart.

> *Au revoir*, dear Mother. I kiss you tenderly; how I love you.
>
> Your little daughter, Thérésita.[89]

Thérèse's affection toward Mother Marie de Gonzague is evident in this *Letter* 9. She ends her letter by saying "I kiss you tenderly; how I love you." Unfortunately, only two letters of Thérèse to the Prioress Mother Marie de Gonzague have been preserved: her *Letter* 9 and her *Letter* 190 (June 29, 1896). Whereas, fifteen letters from the Prioress to Thérèse have been preserved, as well as nine holy cards or images.[90] The Prioress sometimes alludes to Thérèse's letters to her, and therefore we know that Thérèse wrote to her, but her letters were unfortunately not conserved.[91] And so, Thérèse felt a special attraction and tie with the Prioress, as a spiritual mother, since her ninth year of age. The Prioress always encouraged her in her vocation

---

89 *General Correspondence, Vol. I*, trans. John Clarke, OCD, 9.

90 The Prioress wrote seven letters and sent three holy cards to Thérèse before her entrance into Carmel.

91 *Sainte Thérèse de l'Enfant-Jésus et de la Sainte-Face, Nouvelle Édition du Centenaire: Édition critique des Œuvres Complètes, Correspondance générale*, vol. 2: 1890–1897, 2nd rev. ed., 1438–40.

to Carmel, and it was she—Mother Marie de Gonzague—who gave permission for her to enter at fifteen years of age, finally putting an end to the quarrels between the various Superiors about Thérèse's precocious entrance into Carmel. The bishop had placed the matter in the Prioress's hands, who declared herself favorable to Thérèse's youthful vocation.

4. Thérèse's fraternal charity toward sinners and priests

Before speaking of Thérèse's fraternal charity during her years as a nun in the Lisieux Carmel, however, I must mention two privileged categories of persons who received, in a particular way, the benefits of her fraternal charity: sinners and priests. In fact, Thérèse had contact with both sinners and priests before her entrance into Carmel, and her fraternal charity toward them will prove fundamental to her religious life and to her spiritual experience in general. In her *Manuscript* A, Thérèse would later recall the reason why she had entered Carmel: "I had declared at the feet of Jesus-Victim, in the examination preceding my profession, what I had come to Carmel for: 'I came to save souls and especially to pray for priests'" (cf. Ms A, 69v°). Her sister Céline (Sr. Geneviève of the Holy

Face) specified, years later, that in the canonical examination before one's Profession, each nun answered freely regarding the motives of their entrance into Carmel. So Thérèse's response to "save souls" and "especially to pray for priests" was all hers, according to Céline.

Thérèse herself, in her *Manuscript* A, specifies the moment in which her zeal—that is, her charity—for the salvation of souls was enkindled. When describing what she defines as "the grace of my complete conversion," on Christmas Eve 1886, Thérèse wrote: "I felt *charity* enter into my soul, and the need to forget myself and to please others; since then I've been happy!" Immediately afterward, that is, in the very next sentence, she continued:

> One Sunday, looking at a picture of Our Lord on the Cross, I was struck by the blood flowing from one of the divine hands. I felt a great pang of sorrow when thinking this blood was falling to the ground without anyone's hastening to gather it up. I was resolved to remain in spirit at the foot of the Cross and to receive the divine dew. I understood I was then to pour it out upon souls [. . .].

> As yet, it was not the souls of priests that attracted me, but those of *great sinners*; I *burned* with the desire to snatch them from the eternal flames.[92]

Thérèse continues in her account, describing her prayer for the conversion of Henri Pranzini, a notorious murderer condemned to death at the Guillotine, whom she defines as her "first child." (In fact, for Thérèse, we cannot speak of "fraternal charity" without speaking, contemporarily, of her "maternal charity.") I was saying earlier that Thérèse had contact with both sinners and priests before her entrance into Carmel. Speaking of priests, it is certain that Thérèse had various contacts with them as a child. This is obvious, for the fact that she would go to Mass every Sunday with her family. In the Martin and Guérin families, in which Thérèse grew up, priests were held in the highest consideration. Céline (Sr. Geneviève of the Holy Face) would later testify in the Apostolic Process for Thérèse's canonization, regarding her father Louis Martin's respect for priests: "His respect for priests was so great that I've never seen anything like it. I

[92] *Story of a Soul*, trans. John Clarke, OCD, study ed. Marc Foley, OCD, "Autobiographical Manuscript dedicated to Mother Agnes of Jesus," 45.

remember that, being little, I used to think that priests were gods, so accustomed was I to seeing them placed outside the common rank."[93] Thérèse heard about priests not only in the Martin homestead; also during her lessons with Madame Pâpinau—her private tutor as a child—her mother Madame Cochain would often receive guests at home.

"Who could believe it! In this antiquely furnished room, surrounded as I was by text books and copy-books, I was often present at the visits of all types of persons; priests, ladies, young girls, etc." (Ms A, 39v°–40r°), Thérèse wrote in her *Manuscript* A.

Priests would also pay visits to the Martins. We know it from Thérèse, again in her *Manuscript* A:

> It was on Wednesday also that Father Ducellier came to pay a visit. Victoire told him nobody was home except Thérèse, and so he came out into the *kitchen* to see me and look over my homework; I was very proud to receive my *confessor*, for I

---

[93] See Sr. Geneviève of the Holy Face, testimony in *Procés de Béatification et Canonisation de Sainte Thérèse de l'Enfant-Jésus et de la Sainte-Face (II – Procès Apostolique et petit procès pour la recherche des écrits de la sainte)* (Rome: Teresianum, 1976), 256.

> had made my first confession to him a short time before. What a sweet memory for me!

Thérèse's experience of priests, then, as a child, was very positive. Only at fourteen years of age, during her pilgrimage to Rome, would she understand that priests, too, are needy of prayers. In occasion of Pope Leo XIII's 50th anniversary of priesthood ordination, a pilgrimage was organized in France to congratulate him. The French pilgrims were 197, of whom 75 were priests! From November 4 to December 2, 1887, Thérèse found herself in close and daily contact with priests.[94] Thérèse spent three paragraphs in her *Manuscript* A to relate her impression of priests, based on her pilgrimage to Rome. It's worth listening to Thérèse's description. She wrote:

> The second experience I had relates to priests. Having never lived close to them, I was not able to understand the principal aim of the reform of Carmel. To pray for sinners attracted me, but to pray for the souls of priests whom I believed to be as pure as crystal seemed puzzling to me!

---

94 Guy Gaucher, *Saint Thérèse of Lisieux: The Story of a Life* (San Francisco: Ignatius Press, 2020), 87.

It's worth noting that this image of priests being "as pure as crystal" probably derived from a book on St. Francis of Assisi that Thérèse had read as a child. Thérèse continued writing in her *Manuscript* A:

> I understood *my vocation* in *Italy* and that's not going too far in search of such useful knowledge. I lived in the company of many *saintly priests* for a month and I learned that, though their dignity raises them above the angels, they are nevertheless weak and fragile men. If *holy priests*, whom Jesus in His gospel calls the "*salt of the earth,*" show in their conduct their extreme need for prayers, what is to be said of those who are tepid? Didn't Jesus say too: "*If the salt loses its savor, wherewith will it be salted?*"
>
> How beautiful is the vocation, O Mother, which has as its aim the *preservation* of the *salt* destined for souls! This is Carmel's vocation since the sole purpose of our prayers and sacrifices is to be the apostle of the *apostles*. We are to pray for them while they are preaching to souls through their words and especially their

> example. I must stop here, for were I to continue I would never come to an end![95]

5. Thérèse's experience of fraternal charity as a Carmelite religious: her "first steps"

Like Thérèse, we too must stop here in our examination of Thérèse's fraternal charity *before* her entrance into Carmel, and focus on her fraternal charity *during* her years as a nun in the monastery.

It must be said that Thérèse's charity did not stop at the frontiers of any category of persons; I focused my university course—and we're focusing this chapter—on what seemed to me as the most important categories of persons toward whom Thérèse demonstrated her fraternal charity; however, *her charity really had no limits.* Céline (Sr. Geneviève of the Holy Face) later testified for her sister's Process of Beatification:

> Sister Thérèse's love for the poor was quite touching. As a child, she had the honor of handing them the alms, and she insisted on it. She approached them with

95 *Story of a Soul,* trans. John Clarke, OCD, study ed. Marc Foley, OCD, "Autobiographical Manuscript dedicated to Mother Agnes of Jesus," 56.

such affection and respect that one would be tempted to think it was the poor person that was doing her a favor. In Carmel, she would have liked to be infirmarian, because that was the job that required most dedication [. . .].

The Servant of God used to call Pranzini "her child." Later, in Carmel, whenever she received some money on her feast day, she used to get Mother Prioress's permission to use it to get a Mass said. She would then whisper to me: "It's for my child; he must need it after all he's done. I must not abandon him now." After this memorable victory [in her adolescence, of Pranzini's conversion], Thérèse's zeal spread like a forest fire. She undertook to convert a woman who sometimes came to work for us, a complete heathen. She also instructed two poor girls in the faith. It was delightful to listen to her talking about God, and the children listened to her with rapt attention. Later, in Carmel, I saw her furtively

> slip some medals into the overcoats of the workers as they left the convent.[96]

Céline mentions, in this passage of her testimony, Thérèse's charity toward the poor; the sick and the needy; a notorious sinner, Pranzini; a woman who worked for their family; two poor uneducated girls; and even the workers who would enter the Lisieux Carmel to fix up things and take care of practical jobs. In other words, Thérèse focused her charity not only upon certain categories, but upon everyone with whom she would come into contact with. But let's focus now on Thérèse's charity toward her own nun-sisters.

Thérèse would later admit to her sister Pauline, in her *Manuscript* A: "I found the religious life to be *exactly* as I had imagined it, no sacrifice astonished me and yet, as you know, dear Mother, my first steps met with more thorns than roses!"

Now, what were these "thorns" that Thérèse mentions here? They were, of course, the various causes of her sufferings; and her nun-sisters were certainly among those causes. The "Little Flower" shows us, in this context, a portrait of her interior struggle with

---

[96] *St. Thérèse of Lisieux by Those Who Knew Her: Testimonies from the Process of Beatification*, ed. C. O'Mahony (Dublin: Veritas Publications, 2015), 129, 131.

her nun-sisters' faults and criticisms, in her *Letter* 74. She wrote this note to Sr. Agnes of Jesus (Pauline), on January 6, 1889, about nine months after her entrance into the Lisieux Carmel. Thérèse does not hide from her sister the struggle she was facing in trying to overcome her natural sensations and antipathies toward some of her other nun-sisters. She wrote:

> Ask Jesus to make me generous during my retreat. He is riddling me with *pinpricks*; the poor little ball is exhausted. All over it has very little holes which make it suffer more than if it had only one large one! . . . Nothing near Jesus. Aridity! . . . Sleep! . . . But at least there is silence! . . . Silence does good to the soul . . . But creatures! Oh! creatures! . . . The little ball shudders from them! . . . Understand Jesus's little toy! . . . When it is the sweet Friend who punctures His ball Himself, suffering is only sweetness, His hand is *so gentle*! . . . But creatures! . . . Those who surround me are very good, but there is something, I don't know what, that repels me! . . . I cannot give you any explanation. Understand your little soul. I am, however,

> VERY *happy*, happy to suffer what Jesus wants me to suffer. If He doesn't directly puncture His little ball, it is really He who directs the hand that punctures it![97]

One of the sisters who was "puncturing" the little ball—Thérèse—with "pin-pricks," was Sister Saint Vincent de Paul. The commentary of Thérèse's *Letters*, in the New Edition for the Centenary, says:

> This Sister [Saint Vincent de Paul], who was very intelligent but somewhat eccentric, hid a kind heart under a very rough exterior. She never had any sympathy for Thérèse, who was always slow and clumsy in doing anything of a practical nature. Sister St. Vincent de Paul directed many biting remarks at Thérèse, speaking loud enough for Thérèse to hear these remarks. However, Thérèse always answered with a smile. After some years of acting in this way, this Sister did not hesitate to pay respect to Thérèse's extraordinary virtue.[98]

---

[97] *General Correspondence, Vol. II*, trans. John Clarke, OCD, 74.

[98] *General Correspondence, Vol. II*, trans. John Clarke, OCD, 76.

6. Further developments of Thérèse's fraternal charity in the Lisieux Carmel

In the light of this testimony regarding Sister St. Vincent de Paul, let's take a closer look now at the various testimonies of those who lived close to Thérèse in the Lisieux Carmel. Through their testimonies, we can have a privileged and up-close view of Thérèse's fraternal charity "put into practice," as it were. Let's listen, first of all, to her sister Céline (Sr. Geneviève of the Holy Face), who recounts about Thérèse's novitiate:

> From the time she [Thérèse] entered Carmel (1888) until the day I entered it myself (September 1894), [. . .] I saw her at the parlor every eight days, like my other Carmelite sisters. I learned in these interviews that my little sister had much to suffer in the novitiate. Above all, my sister Pauline (Mother Agnes of Jesus) would tell me her displeasure at seeing our little sister badly cared for, exposed to the opposition of many and scolded for no reason. Thérèse then with an angelic air consoled her [Pauline], assured her that she was not unhappy and that she had everything she needed to live. I still

> see her [Thérèse], pale, but saintly joyful to suffer for the good Lord. From these conversations at the parlor it emerged that the main causes of these trials were: 1st: an almost uninterrupted state of dryness in prayer; 2nd: the indiscretion of some nuns who abused her heroic patience. Seeing her so sweet, without ever complaining, all the leftover food was passed on to this child, who should have been well fed instead. Several times she had on her plate nothing but a few heads of herring or some leftovers reheated for several days in a row; 3rd: the quite defective government of the community by Mother Marie de Gonzague, whose unstable and bizarre character made the nuns suffer greatly.[99]

Céline stated that, according to Pauline's recounts to her during her visits in the parlor, Thérèse was "badly cared for, exposed to the opposition of many and scolded for no reason." She was also given all

---

[99] *I Testimoni di Teresa di Gesù Bambino dai Processi di Beatificazione e Canonizzazione*, trans. Suor Amata Ruffinengo (Rome: Edizioni OCD, 2004), 115. (Translation mine.)

the leftovers but she never complained. Let's listen, instead, to one of Thérèse's novices, Sr. Martha of Jesus. Désirée Cauvin—her secular name—was an orphan of both parents and had grown up in various orphanages. She was, as a consequence, emotionally unbalanced; all the nuns feared her violent temper and outlashes of anger. At the same time, she was a "generous and tireless worker, and tried hard, with Thérèse's help, to overcome her temper."[100] Sr. Martha of Jesus testified:

> In her great charity she always found an excuse for those who hurt her, by looking at their intentions, and always took care to be very nice to them. One day I asked her: "How come you always smile so sweetly when Sister X speaks to you? It cannot be because of any attraction because she is always making you suffer." She answered: "That is precisely why I love her, and why I show her so much affection; how could I prove I loved Jesus if I behaved otherwise toward those who hurt me?"

---

[100] Introduction to Sr. Martha of Jesus's testimony, in *St. Thérèse of Lisieux by Those Who Knew Her*, ed. Christopher O'Mahony, 216.

I must bear special testimony to the Servant of God's dealings with myself. She was kindness and charity itself to me; only in heaven will it be realized how much she did for me, and the lengths to which she carried her self-sacrifice on my behalf. I inflicted a great deal of suffering on her through my difficult temperament. But I can honestly say that she always remained calm and kind. I would even go so far as to say that the more I made her suffer, the more she seemed to show me preference and kindness. She never rejected me, in spite of the frequency of my visits; I never noticed even the slightest annoyance in the way she received me. Through her admirable virtues I came to love her dearly. Still, I was sometimes a bit jealous, and would get angry when she called attention to my shortcomings. On such occasions I used to go away and refuse to speak to her. But such was her charity that she always sought me out to try and help me, and her gentleness never failed to win me over.

One day I was upset and said some very hurtful things to her. She just went on talking calmly and gently, asking me to help her with some work she had to do. I gave in, still muttering to myself at the inconvenience she was causing me. Then I thought I would see how far her patience could be stretched, so, to try her virtue, I decided not to answer when she spoke to me. But I failed to upset her, and ended up asking her to forgive me for being so rude. Sister Thérèse did not scold me, nor did she say a word to hurt me; she just encouraged me to be more obliging in future, and taught me the error of my ways. Her charity towards me never ceases to amaze me, and I have often wondered what could make her so interested in a poor lay-sister. I can find no words adequate to express the self-sacrifice with which she attended to my spiritual welfare.[101]

---

[101] *St. Thérèse of Lisieux by Those Who Knew Her*, ed. Christopher O'Mahony, 219–20.

7. Thérèse's own understanding of her personal experience of fraternal charity

After listening to some of Thérèse's nun-sisters and their accounts of her fraternal charity, let's listen briefly now to Thérèse herself, and her own words on fraternal charity. In her *Manuscript* C, Thérèse wrote:

> Mother, when reading what I have just written, you could believe that the practice of charity is not difficult for me. It is true; for several months now I no longer have to struggle to practice this beautiful virtue. I don't mean by this that I no longer have any faults; ah! I am too imperfect for that. But I mean that I don't have any trouble in rising when I have fallen because in a certain combat I won a great victory; and the heavenly militia now comes to my aid since it cannot bear seeing me defeated after having seen me victorious in the glorious battle I am going to try to describe.
>
> There is in the community a sister who has the faculty of displeasing me in everything, in her ways, her words, her character, everything seems *very*

disagreeable to me. And still, she is a holy religious who must be very pleasing to God. Not wishing to give in to the natural antipathy I was experiencing, I told myself that charity must not consist in feelings but in works; then I set myself to doing for this sister what I would do for the person I loved the most. Each time I met her I prayed to God for her, offering Him all her virtues and merits. I felt this was pleasing to Jesus, for there is no artist who doesn't love to receive praise for his works, and Jesus, the artist of souls, is happy when we don't stop at the exterior, but, penetrating into the inner sanctuary where He chooses to dwell, we admire its beauty. I wasn't content simply with praying very much for this sister who gave me so many struggles, but I took care to render her all the services possible, and when I was tempted to answer her back in a disagreeable manner, I was content with giving her my most friendly smile, and with changing the subject of the conversation, for the Imitation says: "*It is better to leave each one in his own opinion than to enter into arguments.*"

Frequently, when I was at recreation (I mean during the work periods) and had occasion to work with this sister, I used to run away like a deserter whenever my struggles became too violent. As she was absolutely unaware of my feelings for her, never did she suspect the motives for my conduct and she remained convinced that her character was very pleasing to me. One day at recreation she asked in almost these words: "Would you tell me, Sister Thérèse of the Child Jesus, what attracts you so much toward me; every time you look at me, I see you smile?" Ah! what attracted me was Jesus hidden in the depths of her soul; Jesus who makes sweet what is most bitter. I answered that I was smiling because I was happy to see her (it is understood that I did not add that this was from a spiritual standpoint).[102]

[102] Autobiographical Manuscript dedicated to Mother Marie de Gonzague, in *Story of a Soul: The Autobiography of Saint Thérèse of Lisieux*, trans. John Clarke, OCD, study ed. Marc Foley, OCD (Washington, D.C.: ICS Publications, 2019), 13–14.

Thérèse had understood—as she wrote only a few pages earlier in her *Manuscript* C—that "charity must not remain hidden in the bottom of the heart" and that, as she wrote, "my love was not to be expressed only in words, for *It is not those who say: 'Lord, Lord!' who will enter the kingdom of heaven, but those who do the will of my Father in heaven*" (cf. Ms C, 11v°.12r°). So Thérèse made sure to overcome her natural feelings and to demonstrate explicitly and in concrete ways—for example, with her best smile—her love for Jesus through her charity toward her nun-sisters.

It's important to remember, as well, that almost all of Thérèse's writings were done either through obedience—for example, her *Manuscripts* A and C—or because of a request on behalf of one of her nun-sisters, or otherwise as a gift for one or another of her nun-sisters, for their feast days or name days or Profession days, etc. This applies especially for Thérèse's *Poems* (almost all of them), but also for her *Plays*, written to cheer and give joy to her nun-sisters at recreation and for special feast days. The same could be said, as well, of various of Thérèse's *Prayers*, written to help or to please one or another of her nun-sisters. There's no time nor space now to analyze all of Thérèse's *Poems*, nor her *Plays* or *Prayers*. We'll have to content ourselves with Thérèse's words—in her *Manuscript* C—which, in some way, reassume and synthesize her whole experience and teaching on fraternal charity, especially as regards her nun-sisters. She wrote: "Yes, I feel it, when I am charitable, it is Jesus alone who is acting in me, and the more united I am to Him, the more also do I love my sisters."

8. The vast extension of Thérèse's charity, especially toward sinners and priests

Thérèse's fraternal charity, then, was put to the test and developed thanks to her nun-sisters; yet, it certainly did not stop there. Her fraternal charity reached out, in a special way, toward sinners and priests.

Thérèse often wrote about priests and the importance of prayer for priests in her vast correspondence with her sister and "pen-pal" Céline. While commiserating and encouraging Céline in her difficulties—Céline had moved in the meantime, together with Léonie, to Caen, to be closer to their father recovered in the psychiatric ward of the *Bon Sauveur* hospital—Thérèse concluded her letter:

> Céline, during the SHORT MOMENTS [of this life] that *remain to us*, let us not lose our time . . . let us save souls . . . souls are being lost like flakes of snow, and Jesus weeps, and we . . . we are thinking of our sorrow without consoling our

> Fiancé . . . Oh, Céline, let us live for souls . . . let us be apostles . . . let us save especially the souls of priests; these souls should be more transparent than crystal. . . Alas, how many bad priests, priests who are not holy enough . . . Let us pray, let us suffer for them, and, on the last day, Jesus will be grateful. We shall give Him souls! . . . Céline, do you understand the cry of my soul?[103]

In the years 1889-1890, the "cry of her soul," to Céline, often repeats itself: "I feel that Jesus is asking *both of us* to quench *His thirst* by giving Him souls, the souls of *priests* especially".[104] "Céline, let us pray for priests, ah, pray for them. May our life be consecrated for them; Jesus makes me feel every day that He wills this from the both of us" (LT 108).[105] "Dear Céline, I *always* have the same thing to say to you. Ah! Let us

---

[103] St. Thérèse of Lisieux, *General Correspondence*, vol. 2: 1890–1897, Letter 94 (July 14, 1889).

[104] St. Thérèse of Lisieux, *General Correspondence*, vol. 2: 1890–1897, Letter 96 (October 15, 1889).

[105] St. Thérèse of Lisieux, *General Correspondence*, vol. 2: 1890–1897, Letter 108 (July 18, 1890).

pray for priests; each day shows how few the friends of Jesus are."[106]

Thérèse also expresses the importance of her fraternal charity toward priests in her poetry. In what is considered her most important poem, *Poem* 17, "Living on Love," Thérèse wrote:

> Living on love, O my Divine Master, Is begging you to spread your Fire
>
> In the holy, sacred souls of your Priest.
>
> May he be purer than a seraphim in Heaven! . . . Ah! glorify your Immortal Church!
>
> Jesus, do not be deaf to my sighs.
>
> I, her child, sacrifice myself for her, I live on Love.

In a poem dedicated to the nuns who served as sacristans in the monastery (*The Sacristans of Carmel*), Thérèse wrote:

> Sublime mission of the Priest,
>
> You become our mission here below.

[106] St. Thérèse of Lisieux, *General Correspondence*, vol. 2: 1890–1897, Letter 122 (October 14, 1890).

Transformed by the Divine Master, It is
He who guides our steps.

We must help the apostles By our prayers,
our love. Their battlefields are ours.
For them we fight each day.

The hidden God of the tabernacle Who
also hides in our hearts,

O what a miracle! At our voice Deigns to
pardon sinners!

Our happiness and our glory Is to work
for Jesus.

His beautiful Heaven is the ciborium We
want to fill with souls!

Thérèse knew that her task of praying for priests was arduous; but she also knew that she was not alone. Turning to the Blessed Virgin Mary in her *Poem* 49, "To Our Lady of Perpetual Help," she wrote: "When I'm struggling, O my dear Mother,/ You strengthen my heart in the fight,/ For you know, at the evening of this life/ I want to offer Priests to the Lord! . . ." (cf. P 49).

Thérèse had always desired—as had her parents before her—to have brothers who would have become missionary priests. When Zélie was pregnant with Thérèse, she had believed that Thérèse was a boy (because of the baby's extraordinary strength) and had wished that her child would become a missionary priest. God was faithful to Thérèse and her parents' desires. Not in the way they had thought, but in an even better way. Thérèse would later write, in her *Manuscript* C:

> It is time to resume the story of my brothers who now hold such a large place in my life. Last year at the end of the month of May, I remember how you called me one day before we went to the refectory. My heart was beating very fast when I entered your cell, dear Mother; I was wondering what you could have to tell me since this was the very first time you called me in this way. After having told me to be seated, you asked me: "Will you take charge of the spiritual interests of a missionary who is to be ordained and leave very soon?" And then, Mother, you read this young priest's letter in order that I might know exactly what he was asking. My first sentiment was one of joy which was immediately replaced by fear. I explained, dear Mother, that having

already offered my poor merits for one future apostle, I believed I could not do it for the intentions of another, and that, besides, there were many sisters better than I who would be able to answer his request. All my objections were useless. You told me that one could have several brothers. Then I asked you whether obedience could double my merits. You answered that it could, and you told me several things which made me see that I had to accept a new brother without any scruples. In the bottom of my heart, Mother, I was thinking the same way as you, and since "*the zeal of a Carmelite embraces the whole world*" I hope with the grace of God to be useful to more than *two* missionaries and I could not forget to pray for all without casting aside simple priests whose mission at times is as difficult to carry out as that of apostles preaching to the infidels [. . .]. Well then! This is how I am spiritually united to the apostles whom Jesus has given me as brothers: all that I have, each of them has, and I know very well that God is too

> good to make divisions; He is so rich He can give without any measure everything I ask Him. . . .[107]

Besides charity for priests, as I said before, Thérèse's charity was especially directed, as well, toward sinners. In her *Profession Note*—which she carried on her heart on the day of her Profession (September 8, 1890) and then placed in a pouch, together with other relics and prayers, which she kept always upon her heart, she wrote: "Jesus, allow me to save very many souls; let no soul be damned today; let all the souls in purgatory be saved . . . Jesus, pardon me if I say anything I should not say. I want only to give you joy and to console you" (Pr 2). In this *Prayer* 2, her *Profession Note*, Thérèse's view—her *régard*–already started to resemble that universal view of fraternal charity later expressed in another of her *Prayers*: her *Prayer* 6, *Act of Oblation to Merciful Love*, written between June 9 and 11, 1895. She wrote:

---

[107] Autobiographical Manuscript dedicated to Mother Marie de Gonzague, in *Story of a Soul: The Autobiography of Saint Thérèse of Lisieux*, trans. John Clarke, OCD, study ed. Marc Foley, OCD (Washington, D.C.: ICS Publications, 2019), 33.

> O my God! Most Blessed Trinity, I desire to *Love* you and make you Loved, to work for the glory of Holy Church by saving souls on earth and liberating those suffering in purgatory. I desire to accomplish your will perfectly and to reach the degree of glory you have prepared for me in your kingdom. I desire, in a word, to be a Saint, but I feel my helplessness and I beg you, O my God! to be yourself my Sanctity! [. . .]. I offer you, too, all the merits of the Saints (in Heaven and on earth), their acts of Love, and those of the Holy Angels. Finally, I offer you, O Blessed Trinity! the Love and merits of the Blessed Virgin, my dear Mother [. . .].

Less than a year after making her act of oblation to Merciful Love, Thérèse's almost universal view (of fraternal charity) "zooms" in, so to speak, with great intensity and precision, upon sinners. On Easter Sunday, 1896, Thérèse entered into a deep and dark trial of her faith. While writing about this "trial of faith" in June 1897, in her *Manuscript* C, Thérèse defined sinners as her "brothers." She wrote:

> Your child, however, O Lord, has understood Your divine light, and she begs pardon for her brothers. She is resigned to eat the bread of sorrow as long as You desire it; she does not wish to rise up from this table filled with bitterness at which poor sinners are eating until the day set by You. Can she not say in her name and in the name of her brothers, "*Have pity on us, O Lord, for we are poor sinners!*". Oh! Lord, send us away justified. May all those who were not enlightened by the bright flame of faith one day see it shine. O Jesus! if it is needful that the table soiled by them be purified by a soul who loves You, then I desire to eat this bread of trial at this table until it pleases You to bring me into Your bright kingdom. The only grace I ask of You is that I never offend You!

Thérèse's charity was growing more and more, even to the point of an intimate participation in the innocent sufferings of Christ for the sins of others: He is the Lamb of God, who takes upon Himself the sins of the world. Thérèse's charity, indeed, participated in that of God's, and thus knew no bounds. Less than a year before, in her *Manuscript* B, Thérèse had already expressed such unlimited charity, toward all men and women of all times. She had written:

> *Charity* gave me the key to my *vocation.* I understood that if the Church had a body composed of different members, the most necessary and most noble of all could not be lacking to it, and so I understood that the Church *had a Heart and that this Heart was BURNING WITH LOVE. I understood it was Love alone* that made the Church's members act, that if *Love* ever became extinct, apostles would not preach the gospel and martyrs would not shed their blood. I understood that LOVE COMPRISED ALL VOCATIONS, THAT LOVE WAS EVERYTHING, THAT IT EMBRACED ALL TIMES AND PLACES . . . IN A WORD, THAT IT WAS ETERNAL! Then, in the excess of my delirious joy, I cried out: "O Jesus, my Love . . . my vocation, at last I have found it . . . MY VOCATION IS LOVE! Yes, I have found my place in the

Church and it is You, O my God, who have given me this place; in the heart of the Church, my Mother, I shall be *Love*. Thus I shall be everything, and thus my dream will be realized.[108]

[108] Letter to Sister Marie of the Sacred Heart, in *Story of a Soul: The Autobiography of Saint Thérèse of Lisieux*, trans. John Clarke, OCD, study ed. Marc Foley, OCD (Washington, D.C.: ICS Publications, 2019), 3.

St. Thérèse in the year 1896 (at 23 years of age). The book that Thérèse is holding in her right hand had been given to her by her missionary brother Adolphe Roulland. It speaks of the mission in Su-Tchuen, China, where he was destined as a missionary. Thérèse is holding a parchment in her left hand, on which she had written a phrase of St. Teresa of Avila: "I would give a thousand lives to save a soul."

CHAPTER SIX

Thérèse's "Passion" and "Death of Love"

1. Introduction: Christ's Paschal Mystery and Thérèse

The title of this sixth and last chapter of our book on Thérèse refers to Thérèse's sickness and death. However, I preferred calling it her "Passion" and her "Death of Love." These terms refer, of course, to Christ's experience. Even her "death of love," a concept expounded upon by St. John of the Cross, Thérèse was to reinterpret in the light of Christ's sufferings and death. In fact, Christ's Paschal Mystery—His Passion, Death, and Resurrection—is the most correct and fundamental key for understanding Thérèse's sickness, death, and entrance into eternal life. Now, I won't be speaking here of Christ's Passion, Death, and Resurrection, as I assume that you all have not only read, but in some way studied and meditated upon the Gospels and, of course, lived in first person the Liturgy of the Church, most especially the Holy Triduum and Easter Sunday. So, let's skip directly to Thérèse's experience; but, keep in mind the Paschal Mystery of Christ.

2. Understanding Thérèse's "Passion" and Death

The best book, by far—in my opinion—on the topic we'll be considering now is *The Passion of Thérèse of Lisieux*, written by the Theresian expert, Msgr. Guy Gaucher.[109] I also have two other personal experiences, which I lived recently, and which have guided me in my personal understanding of Thérèse's sickness and death: that is, the sickness and death of my Foundress († July 12, 2020) and the sickness and death of my sister Susy († December 8, 2023). Studying Thérèse (before and especially after their deaths), I have found many resemblances between her and them. Sickness and death is something that belongs, sooner or later, to every human experience, and thus there are common elements to be found in every person's sickness and death; moreover, I found many resemblances, too,

[109] Guy Gaucher, *The Passion of Thérèse of Lisieux, 4 April–30 September 1897* (New York: The Crossroad Publishing Company, 1990).

regarding their spiritual experience and their life of faith, compared to that of Thérèse. I won't be speaking of this at length, but I thought that it was important to mention. In fact, the death of saints, like Thérèse—and, first and foremost, that of the Holy One *par excellence*, Jesus Christ, the Son of God—helps us to better understand and correctly interpret the death of our loved ones . . . and even our own death. They also teach us *how* to die.

3. Death in the Martin family

Thérèse was quite familiar with death. In fact, she herself eluded death various times in her life. She almost died several times in the first weeks and months of her life; she refused her mother Zélie's breast and risked to die of enteritis, that is, inflammation of the small intestine. The Martin family had already lost four children in the same way: Hélène, Joseph Louis, Joseph John-Baptist, and Mélanie. They were often spoke about in the Martin homestead. (Louis Martin never fully overcame the loss of his beloved Helen, who had died at five years of age.) Already familiar with death, at four years of age Thérèse lost her mother Zélie. The unbereaved loss of her mother would later catalyze—after the shock of losing suddenly her "second mother,"

Pauline—that "strange sickness" of Thérèse, healed by the Blessed Virgin Mary on Pentecost Sunday 1883, at ten years of age. Her family had feared the worst: it had seemed that Thérèse would die. And maybe she would have, had the Blessed Virgin not intervened with her "ravishing smile." Shortly after her entrance into Carmel, her dear father Louis started suffering, in June of 1888, the first signs of his illness, which would later lead to his death on July 29, 1894.

4. Thérèse's first symptoms . . .

Thérèse had eluded death various times in her childhood, I was saying before. Just as her dear father was nearing *his* death,[110] Thérèse started showing signs of her illness, which would prove to be fatal. She was to reach her father, in Heaven, little more than three years later. In June of 1894, we have the first evidence of a medical treatment given to Thérèse.[111] But, in

---

[110] St. Thérèse of Lisieux, *General Correspondence*, vol. 2: 1890–1897, trans. John Clarke, O.C.D. (Washington, DC: ICS Publications, 2014), 856. ("Repeated heart attacks, in May and June [1894], announced the approaching end of Mr. Martin.")

[111] Guy Gaucher, *The Passion of Thérèse of Lisieux, 4 April–30 September 1897* (New York: The Crossroad Publishing Company, 1990), 36.

reality, Thérèse had always had fragile health. Pauline Martin (Mother Agnes of Jesus) would later write about Thérèse in her childhood years: "She was sick every winter. A slight cold would bring on a high temperature and great difficulty in breathing."[112] This "difficulty in breathing" had been present since Thérèse's infancy. Her mother Zélie, in a letter dated to November 12, 1876—when Thérèse was only three years old—wrote: "I am worried about my little Thérèse. For several months she has had difficulty in breathing that is not normal. As soon as she begins to walk a little quicker, a strange whistling sound can be heard in her chest." Again, on January 8, 1887, Zélie wrote about Thérèse: "My little Thérèse is sick. I am worried about her. She frequently suffers from colds that cause difficulty in breathing. It usually lasts for two days." And Céline would later recount: "As a child, Thérèse could not run because she easily became short of breath."[113] No wonder, then, that Thérèse would later die of a sickness which affected her lungs. Guy Gaucher, commenting on Thérèse's environment and

---

[112] Guy Gaucher, *The Passion of Thérèse of Lisieux*, 35. (Quotation found here.)

[113] Guy Gaucher, *The Passion of Thérèse of Lisieux*, 35. (These quotations can be found here.)

her susceptibility to falling ill, wrote in his book *The Passion of Thérèse of Lisieux*:

> The climate of Lisieux, and in particular that of the Carmel, situated on the banks of the Orbiquet [river], was hardly suitable for a young adolescent who had a rather weak throat, was subject to winter colds, and who had suffered earlier from "difficulty in breathing." To an unfavorable geographical position must be added the very strict regime of the Carmelite life at the end of the 19th Century: the continual cold that made Thérèse suffer "even to the point of dying from it," the poor food, the prolonged fasts and lack of sleep. Conditions not helpful to the physical growth of a young girl between fifteen and twenty.[114]

On July 1, 1894, Thérèse was examined by her cousin-in-law, Dr. Francis La Néele. Her cousin Marie Guérin had written in a letter to her sister Jeanne (who was married to Dr. Francis), a few days before: "At Carmel, they expect Francis on Sunday, who will see

---

[114] Guy Gaucher, *The Passion of Thérèse of Lisieux*, 35–36.

Thérèse, who has a persistent sore throat, hoarse voice, and some pains in her *chest.*"[115] A few days before, Céline had written to Thérèse: "Above all, take care of yourself, this is a duty of conscience."[116] A few months later, Thérèse's health was not improving; her family was starting to get alarmed. Her cousin Marie Guérin wrote to Céline in October 1894, that is a month after her [Céline's] entrance into the Lisieux Carmel (September 14, 1894):

> May little Thérèse take good care of herself; I found her voice very much changed yesterday, so I spoke to [Dr.] Francis about her. It is absolutely necessary that she take care of herself ENERGETICALLY. For the moment there is nothing serious, but it can become so from one day to the next, and then there will be no longer any remedy. Right now she can very well be cured, but for this she must take care of herself without letting up. Let her

---

[115] St. Thérèse of Lisieux, *General Correspondence*, vol. 2: 1890–1897, trans. John Clarke, O.C.D. (Washington, DC: ICS Publications, 2014), 870.

[116] St. Thérèse of Lisieux, *General Correspondence*, vol. 2: 1890–1897, LC 159, trans. John Clarke, O.C.D., 869.

> especially use a lot of *gillete* [a medicinal spray] [. . .]. Little Thérèse would have to be very obedient to the doctor. Francis is a specialist for these illnesses [of the respiratory system], so I believe him and have great confidence in him. He cured Mr. Ferouelle from a sickness which was very grave, he will also cure little Thérèse. I am going to promise a very large sum to my little St. Anthony purse so that in six months my little sister may be entirely cured and in good health.[117]

5. Thérèse's fragile health: a short lifespan?

Thérèse's entourage was starting to realize, then, that "for the moment there is nothing serious, but it can become so from one day to the next." Dr. Francis was right. Not only her family members, but especially Thérèse herself was starting to realize that she may not live a long life. We've already examined how this awareness helped to catalyze Thérèse's discovery of her

[117] St. Thérèse of Lisieux, *General Correspondence*, vol. 2: 1890–1897, LC 160a, LD (from Marie Guérin to Sister Marie of the Holy Face [Céline Martin], in LC 159), trans. John Clarke, O.C.D., 892.

"Little Way." She desired to become a great saint, yet she had little time left to live; and she was still so "weak and imperfect." How could she become a saint in a small amount of time? In the Holy Scriptures, Thérèse was to find her answer, which she would later express in the following terms: "The elevator which must raise me to heaven is Your arms, O Jesus! And for this I had no need to grow up, but rather I had to remain *little* and become this more and more" (cf. Ms C, 2v°–3r°).

6. Thérèse and the "death of love"

Only a few months later, Thérèse started writing explicitly about her desire for a "death of love." In her *Poem* 17 (February 26, 1895), she wrote:

> "Living on Love, what strange folly!"
>
> The world says to me, "Ah! stop your singing, Don't waste your perfumes, your life. Learn to use them well . . .".
>
> Loving you, Jesus, is such a fruitful loss! . . . All my perfumes are yours forever.
>
> I want to sing on leaving this world:
>
> "I'm dying of love!".

Dying of Love is a truly sweet martyrdom, And that is the one I wish to suffer.

O Cherubim! Tune your lyre,

For I sense my exile is about to end! . . . Flame of Love, consume me unceasingly.

Life of an instant, your burden is so heavy to me! Divine Jesus, make my dream come true:

To die of Love! . . .

Dying of Love is what I hope for. When I shall see my bonds broken, My God will be my Great Reward.

I don't desire to possess other goods.

I want to be set on fire with his Love.

I want to see Him, to unite myself to Him forever.

That is my Heaven . . . that is my destiny:

Living on Love!!!

St. John of the Cross's influence is clear in this *Poem* 17 of Thérèse, "Living on Love!" Thérèse had borrowed, from the library of the monastery, a book containing both *The Spiritual Canticle* and *The Living Flame of Love* of St. John of the Cross. She had done so, most probably, in February of 1889.[118] After the recovery of her dear father Louis in the psychiatric ward of the *Bon Sauveur* hospital in Caen, Thérèse was seeking a guide and an inspiration to better live, together with the suffering Lord, her own personal sufferings. She found response in a growing devotion to the Holy Face of Jesus—and later on, the Suffering Servant of Isaiah—and in St. John of the Cross. It is in the *Living Flame of Love*, in fact, that St. John of the Cross speaks of the "death of love" of those souls who, already mystically espoused to God in this earthly life, have the "veil"—that is, the bond between their body and their soul—ruptured suddenly by a particularly strong visit of the Bridegroom, God. It is that rupture which causes the "death of love." For St. John of the Cross, such a death is accompanied by the most sweet and profound joys, more than any joy experienced by the soul during its earthly life. Thérèse continued to deepen St. John of the Cross for the rest of her life:

---

[118] Joseph Spence, *Un'esperienza sponsale con Dio: l'influsso di san Giovanni della Croce su santa Teresa di Lisieux*, Dissertazione della tesi dottorale (Rome: Teresianum, A.A. 2019–2020), 45–61.

she even read it, underlined it, and marked certain passages of this volume, which she kept on her bedside table in the Infirmary, in the last months of her life! After her *Poem* 17, various other poems echo her desire for a "death of love." "O Jesus! may I die one day/ Of love! . . ." she wrote in her *Poem* 18, "The Canticle of Céline." In her *Poem* 21, composed for the entrance into the Lisieux Carmel of her cousin, Marie Guérin, "Canticle of a Soul Having Found the Place of its Rest!" Thérèse wrote:

> Jesus, in Carmel I want to live,
>
> Since to this oasis your love has called me.
>
> It's there that I want to follow you To love you, to love you and to die. It's there that I want to follow you There, yes, there!

Whereas, in her *Poem* 24, composed for Céline, "Jesus, My Beloved, Remember!" Thérèse encourages her sister to focus not on what she has left and sacrificed for Jesus (comparably very little), but rather on what He left and sacrificed for her! Thérèse wrote, for Céline:

> Remember, Jesus, Word of Life,

How you loved me and even died for me.
    I also want to love you to folly.
I also want to live and die for You.
You know, O my God! all that I desire
Is to make you loved and one day be a
    martyr.
I want to die of love. Lord, my desire,
    Remember.

To "die of love" becomes a veritable refrain, in Thérèse's poems. In her verses, Thérèse feels free to address Jesus not with the formal "*Vous,*" as was custom in prayers, but with the informal and intimate "*Tu.*" In her poetry, Thérèse can express herself freely. And so she does. One more example will suffice: in the night between July 12 and 13, 1897—only a few months before her death—Thérèse composed her last poem, the so-called *Supplementary Poem* 8, "You Who Know my Extreme Littleness." It is a Eucharistic poem. She wrote:

You who know my extreme littleness,
You aren't afraid to lower yourself to me!
    Come into my heart, O white Host

that I love, Come into my heart, it
longs for you!

Ah! I wish that your goodness

Would let me die of love after this favor.
Jesus! Hear the cry of my affection.

Come into my heart!

On July 16, a few days later, Sister Marie of the Eucharist (her cousin Marie Guérin) sang this stanza "with a beautiful, strong voice" prior to Thérèse receiving the Holy Communion in the infirmary. After Communion, "she sang stanza 14 from *Living on Love*: 'Dying of love is a truly sweet martyrdom.'"[119] (In fact, Thérèse composed most of her poetry with the intent of it being sung, adapting the verses to well-known hymns or pious songs from her time period.)

7. The development of Thérèse's fatal sickness

Before speaking of the "death of love," of Thérèse, and her final interpretation of St. John of the Cross's "death of love," we must take a step back in time. We must analyze more closely—even though briefly—the

[119] *The Poetry of Saint Thérèse of Lisieux*, trans. Donald Kinney, O.C.D. (Washington, DC: ICS Publications, 2013), 233.

progression of Thérèse's sickness. From her first symptoms in 1894, Thérèse's health gradually but surely declined. Yet, it was only on Good Friday of 1896—almost two years later—that Thérèse would experience the most significant indication of a severe illness. She would later express this episode in her *Manuscript* C; she wrote:

> On Good Friday, however, Jesus wished to give me the hope of going to see Him soon in heaven. Oh! how sweet this memory really is! After remaining at the tomb until midnight, I returned to our cell, but I had scarcely laid my head upon the pillow when I felt something like a bubbling stream mounting to my lips. I didn't know what it was, but I thought that perhaps I was going to die and my soul was flooded with joy. However, as our lamp was extinguished, I told myself I would have to wait until the morning to be certain of my good fortune, for it seemed to me that it was blood I had coughed up. The morning was not long in coming; upon awakening, I thought immediately of the joyful thing that I had to learn, and

> so I went over to the window. I was able to see that I was not mistaken. Ah! my soul was filled with a great consolation: I was interiorly persuaded that Jesus, on the anniversary of His own death, wanted to have me hear His first call. *It was like a sweet and distant murmur that announced the Bridegroom's arrival.*[120]

Thérèse speaks here of being "flooded with joy," at the thought of her nearing death. "It was like a sweet and distant murmur that announced the Bridegroom's arrival," she wrote, alluding to Jesus's parable of the ten virgins awaiting the Bridegroom's arrival. And so it truly was. The day after, she had her second coughing-up (hemoptysis) of blood. However, her sensible joy, at the thought of heaven, was soon to end. The day after, the evening of Easter Sunday 1896, Thérèse's soul was plunged into darkness. She would later describe this state of her soul, at length, in her *Manuscript* C:

---

[120] Autobiographical Manuscript dedicated to Mother Marie de Gonzague, in *Story of a Soul: The Autobiography of Saint Thérèse of Lisieux*, trans. John Clarke, OCD, study ed. Marc Foley, OCD (Washington, D.C.: ICS Publications, 2019), 4–5.

> He [Jesus] permitted my soul to be invaded by the thickest darkness, and that the thought of heaven, up until then so sweet to me, be no longer anything but the cause of struggle and torment. This trial was to last not a few days or a few weeks, it was not to be extinguished until the hour set by God Himself and this hour has not yet come.

Thérèse was about to live her "Passion," following her Lord on the way to Calvary. She was to suffer not only in her body, but most especially in her soul. Let's take a quick look at what she suffered in her body. There is no time now for a complete compilation or examination of her physical sufferings and sickness which would lead her to a premature death. In that regard, I again highly recommend Guy Gaucher's excellent book, *The Passion of Thérèse of Lisieux.* I will only mention a few aspects. Thérèse's sickness started progressing ever more quickly in the springtime of 1897, her last year of life. And yet, most of the nuns were not aware of the severity of her disease. Nor did they know exactly what it was. Not even the doctors—Dr. Francis La Néele and the community doctor, Dr. de Cornière—were sure of her diagnosis. Nonetheless,

Thérèse's extreme weakness forced her, in obedience to the Prioress, to slowly withdraw from community tasks and appointments. Referring to that time period, Sr. Mary of the Trinity (one of her novices) would later testify in the Diocesan Process for her Beatification:

> The last day that [Thérèse] could stand on her feet she came to the evening recreation. The Servant of God, having difficulty in breathing and running a temperature, came into the recreation room and came and sat on her heels next to me. She whispered to me: "I have come near you so that you can *guard* me. I feel that I have not the strength to carry on a conversation. Look as if you are talking to me so that others won't come to speak to me. I do feel so sick, but I don't want to tell Mother Agnès [Pauline] yet, she would worry so much! . . . Last evening it took me more than half an hour to get up to my cell, I had to sit down on almost every step of the stairs to get my breath. When I finally reached my cell, I had to make an unbelievable effort to undress. I thought at the time that I would never make it . . .

> if you only knew how powerless we can become through illness!" [121]

Toward the end of May 1897, Thérèse was prescribed with various remedies of that time period, which proved to be completely useless. However, some of them were extremely painful. They included "vesicatories, cough syrup, sedatives, and *pointes de feu.*"[122] The so-called vesicatories were hot-pads which would be placed for hours on the skin of the patient, so as to purposely make the skin blister. The thought was that such a reaction would help to "draw out" the sickness from the patient's body. The worst of the remedies, however, was the *pointes de feu.* That is, the "points of fire." A syringe was heated until it became red-hot; the doctor would then proceed to prick, with the red-hot syringe, the back of the patient. In the Apostolic Process for Thérèse's canonization, Céline would later recount:

> I can still see her [Thérèse] enduring more than five hundred points of fire on

---

[121] Guy Gaucher, *The Passion of Thérèse of Lisieux, 4 April–30 September 1897* (New York: The Crossroad Publishing Company, 1990), 73. (Quotes testimony of Sr. Mary of the Trinity.)

[122] Guy Gaucher, *The Passion of Thérèse of Lisieux*, 73.

> her back (I counted them myself). In the meantime that the doctor [de Cornière] was operating, discussing trivial things with our Mother [Prioress, Marie de Gonzague], the angelic patient was standing, leaning on a table. She was offering, she told me later, her sufferings for souls and thinking of martyrs. After the session [of "*pointes de feu*"], she went up to her cell, without waiting for a word of compassion to be addressed to her, sitting down all trembling on the edge of her straw mattress, and there, endured alone the effect of this painful treatment.[123]

Thérèse's thought of dying a martyr truly did sustain her in the times of her sickness, as Céline testified as regards to this painful episode of *pointes de feu*. The treatments, however, as *useless* and as painful as they were, were still not comparable to the sufferings caused by the sickness itself: tuberculosis. Pauline would later testify that Thérèse never received even one shot of morphine. She did, in the last days of her

---

[123] Joseph Spence, *Un'esperienza sponsale con Dio: l'influsso di san Giovanni della Croce su santa Teresa di Lisieux*, 248. (Quoted from my doctoral thesis.)

life, receive a few spoonfuls of morphine syrup, not nearly as effective as the shots. Nor did she ever receive oxygen. The tuberculosis was slowly but surely eating away at Thérèse's lungs. In her last months, she lost first her right lung; and then her left lung. For the last month of her life, Thérèse had to breathe with one-half of one lung, the left. By her death, that lung was also consumed. In the worst period of her hemoptyses, Thérèse would cough up blood every two or three days: "a generous glassful in a quarter of an hour."[124] It was during the consummation of her left lung that Thérèse, perhaps, suffered the most. In the *Green Notebook*, edited years later by Pauline, she testified:

> On August 22nd [. . .] she [Thérèse] asked that poisonous drugs not be left near her and she advised that they never be left near patients suffering this intense pain which could "make one go out of one's mind and, not knowing what they are doing, they could very well take their own life."[125]

---

[124] Guy Gaucher, *The Passion of Thérèse of Lisieux*, 80.

[125] Guy Gaucher, *The Passion of Thérèse of Lisieux, 4 April–30 September 1897* (New York: The Crossroad Publishing Company, 1990), 88, note "u." (Quotation taken from here.)

Thérèse mentioned her temptations to commit suicide on several occasions. Again, to Pauline, she said: "If I had not the faith, I would have committed suicide without a moment's hesitation."[126] But it was not yet the end. Her infection, after consuming her lungs, soon spread to her intestines.

8. "Love is as strong as death" (Song of Songs 8:6)

Again, there is no time now to make a specific and detailed description of the humiliating and excruciating sufferings of Thérèse. What is most striking, in all of this, is another fact: actually, two other facts. First of all, that the principal cause of Thérèse's sufferings was not that of her body, but that of her soul: her trial of faith, that is of faith in heaven. (See, for example, Thérèse's description of her trial of faith in her *Manuscript* C.) And, then, another fact: that, in all of this—in her martyrdom, in her *Via Crucis*—Thérèse was full of joy. Full of humor. Full of love. There is only one way to truly understand the purity, the candor, the simplicity, the heroism, the love, which had

---

[126] *Yellow Notebook*, 9.22.6 (September 22, 1897). Quotation cited in Guy Gaucher, *The Passion of Thérèse of Lisieux*, 88.

imbibed Thérèse's soul—through the action of the Holy Spirit—and I am not able to express it myself. You'll have to read the *Yellow Notebook* yourself to truly understand. It is a privileged source for seeing Thérèse close-up, as she was, in the last months of her life. It's almost like watching a movie of Thérèse, as she was; and seeing such a little-great saint, close-up, in her Passion and Death of Love, is really something! Sr. Agnes of Jesus (Pauline) collected Thérèse's words and gestures, at her bedside, and wrote them down onto various scraps of paper. She would do so even as Thérèse was speaking, or, at the latest, on the evening of the same day. Shortly after Thérèse's death, Pauline gathered her scraps of paper together and ordered them chronologically, transcribing them into a notebook bound with yellow-colored leather: the *Yellow Notebook*. The source, thus, is trustworthy.

What, then, of Thérèse's "death of love"? Although instructed by St. John of the Cross, the reality of her sickness forced her to re-think things: her experience did not coincide with that described by the Spanish saint. Thérèse turned to the Gospels, and to Jesus's experience; her Crucifix, which she held constantly in her hands during the last months of her illness, and which she often contemplated, gave her the answer to her dilemma. She said to Pauline, on July 4, 1897:

"Our Lord died on the Cross in agony, and yet this is the most beautiful death of love [. . .]. To die of love is not to die in transports. I tell you frankly, it seems to me that this is what I am experiencing."[127]

In a final thought, I will share with you Pauline's recount of Thérèse's last moments. And, I would say, her "death of love." Mother Agnès of Jesus (Pauline) described her sister's death in the following words:

> Her breathing suddenly became weaker and more labored. She fell back on the pillow, her head turned towards the right. The infirmary bell was rung and, to allow the nuns to assemble quickly, Mother Marie de Gonzague said in a loud voice: "Open all the doors." Hardly had the nuns knelt at her bedside when she pronounced very distinctly her final act of love: "Oh! I love Him . . ." she said, looking at her crucifix. Then a moment later: "My God . . . I . . . love you!"
>
> We thought that was the end, when, suddenly, she raised her eyes, eyes that were full of life and shining with an indescribable happiness "surpassing all

[127] *Yellow Notebook*, 7.4.2 (July 4, 1897).

her hopes." Sister Marie of the Eucharist approached with a candle to get a better look at that sublime gaze which lasted for the space of a "Credo." The light from the candle passed back and forth in front of her eyes did not cause any movement in her eye-lids . . . It was twenty-past-seven.

Then she closed her eyes and the whiteness of her face, which had become more accentuated during the ecstasy, returned to normal. She appeared ravishingly beautiful and had a heavenly smile . . . We did not have to close her eyes, for she had closed them herself after the vision. Mother Prioress then had the community retire, and Sister Aimée, Sister Marie of the Sacred Heart and I prepared the Servant of God for burial. Her face had a childlike expression and she didn't seem any more than twelve years old.

When she was dressed and lying on her paillasse, according to the custom of Carmel, before lifting the body, we placed in her hand, together with her crucifix and rosary, a palm branch, and next to her, on a small table, we put the statue of the miraculous Virgin.

The Servant of God retained the expression she had when she died. Her head was turned towards the right and her smile was so marked that we thought she was only asleep and having a happy dream. Her limbs were supple until the coffin was closed.[128]

[128] Guy Gaucher, *The Passion of Thérèse of Lisieux*, 94–95. (Recount quoted here.)

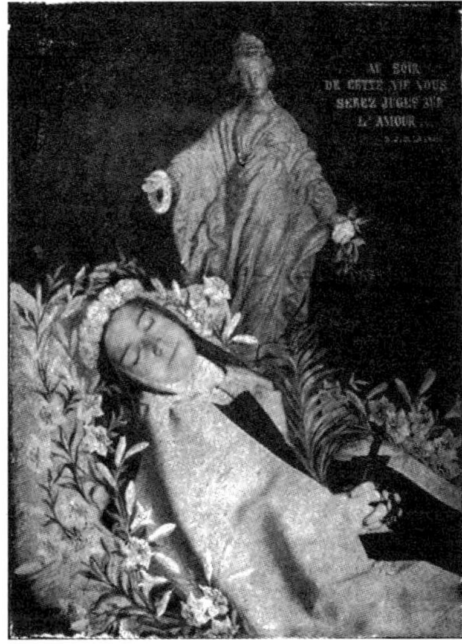

Thérèse shortly after her death.

Her Carmelite sisters arranged her on her deathbed with the lilies and the palm (as a symbol of her "martyrdom"). The Virgin of the Smile was placed behind her.

CONCLUSION

"Who can understand"—the prophet Jeremiah asks—the heart of man? Certainly, a man cannot. "I the LORD search the heart and examine the mind," responds the Lord (cf. Jer. 17:9–10). Thus, only the Lord can truly enter into the sanctuary of the heart of man; only He can define us and give us a new name, or rather "a white stone with a new name written on it, known only to the one who receives it" (Rev. 2:17).

At the end of this booklet on St. Thérèse and her spirituality, we cannot pretend to have truly entered into the center of the sanctuary of Thérèse's heart. Nonetheless, I think that we've come a little closer . . .With the six "keys" provided in this book, I'm confident that we have opened at least six doors—some familiar, most new—that lead closer and closer to Thérèse's heart.

After having examined the development of Thérèse's "Little Way," we then passed on to consider the significance and importance of her religious name, chosen by Thérèse herself, "of the Child Jesus and of the Holy Face." After that, we came to understand how Thérèse's "spousal" relationship with Jesus is in no way marginal: on the contrary, it is her habitual way of relating with Him. A quick glance at Thérèse's spiritual maternity led the way to a deeper understanding of her relationship with the Blessed Virgin Mary, a Mother always by her side. After having considered, at length, Thérèse's relationship with God, it was consequential and necessary to examine her relationship with her neighbor: that is, her "fraternal charity." The last topic, both logically and chronologically, was Thérèse's "Passion" and death, a veritable immersion in Christ's Paschal Mystery.

May these six "keys" help all of us to enter ever more deeply into the heart of Thérèse and, as a result, into the Heart of Christ.

BIBLIOGRAPHY

Sources of Living the Little Way

Gaucher, Guy, in collaboration with the Carmel of Lisieux. *Les Cahiers d'école de Thérèse de Lisieux (1877–1888).* Paris: Cerf, 2008. (The School Notebooks of Thérèse of Lisieux [1877–1888]).

Ruffinengo, Suor Amata, translator. *I Testimoni di Teresa di Gesù Bambino dai Processi di Beatificazione e Canonizzazione.* Roma: Edizioni OCD, 2004.

Procés de Béatification et Canonisation de Sainte Thérèse de l'Enfant-Jésus et de la Sainte-Face. I – Procès Informatif Ordinaire. Roma: Teresianum, 1973. II – Procès Apostolique et petit procès pour la recherche des écrits de la sainte. Roma: Teresianum, 1976.

Sainte Thérèse de l'Enfant-Jesus et de la Sainte-Face, Œuvres complètes (Textes et Dernières Paroles). Lonrai: Éditions du Cerf/Desclée De Brouwer, 1992.

Saint Thérèse of Lisieux. *General Correspondence.* Vol. I, 1877–1890. Translated by John Clarke, O.C.D. Washington, D.C.: ICS Publications, 1982. Vol. II, 1890–1897. Translated by John Clarke, O.C.D. Washington, D.C.: ICS Publications, 1988.

Saint Thérèse of Lisieux. *Her Last Conversations.* Translated by John Clarke, O.C.D. Washington, D.C.: ICS Publications, 1977.

Sainte Thérèse de l'Enfant-Jesus et de la Sainte-Face, "Nouvelle Édition du Centenaire," Édition critique des Œuvres Complètes, 8 vols. Lonrai: Éditions du Cerf/Desclée De Brouwer, 1992. (Critical edition of the complete works, in 8 volumes.)

Sister Geneviève of the Holy Face. *My Sister Saint Thérèse (CSG).* Authorized translation by the Carmelite Sisters of New York of *Conseils et Souvenirs.* Rockford, IL: TAN Books and Publishers, Inc., 1997.

Story of a Soul: The Autobiography of Saint Thérèse of Lisieux. Translated from the original manuscripts by John Clarke, O.C.D. A study edition prepared by Marc Foley, O.C.D. Washington, D.C.: ICS Publications, 2019.

O'Mahony, Christopher, ed. *St. Thérèse of Lisieux by Those Who Knew Her: Testimonies from the Process of Beatification.* Dublin: Veritas Publications, 2016.

Martin, Céline. *Teresa di Lisieux, Consigli e Ricordi.* Roma: Città Nuova Editrice, 2013. (The Italian version of *Conseils et Souvenirs.*)

Gaucher, Guy, O.C.D., general introduction. *The Plays of Saint Thérèse of Lisieux: "Pious Recreations."* Translated by Susan Conroy and David J. Dwyer. Washington, D.C.: ICS Publications, 2008.

Kinney, Donald, O.C.D., translator. *The Poetry of Saint Thérèse of Lisieux: Complete Edition, Texts and Introductions.* Washington, D.C.: ICS Publications, 1996.

Gaucher, Guy, general introduction. *The Prayers of Saint Thérèse of Lisieux.* Translated by Aletheia Kane, O.C.D. Washington, D.C.: ICS Publications, 1997.

Carmel of Lisieux Archives. *https://archives.carmeldelisieux.fr/en/*

Studies on St. Thérèse of the Child Jesus and of the Holy Face

Magisterium

Francis, Pope. *Apostolic Exhortation C'est la confiance on Confidence in the Merciful Love of God for the 150th Anniversary of the Birth of St. Thérèse of the Child Jesus and the Holy Face.* October 15, 2023. https://www.vatican.va/content/francesco/en/apost_exhortations/documents/20231015-santateresa-delbambinogesu.html.

John Paul II, Pope. *Apostolic Letter Divini Amoris Scientia.* October 19, 1997. https://www.vatican.va/content/john-paul-ii/en/apost_letters/1997/documents/hf_jp-ii_apl_19101997_divini-amoris.html.

Benedict XVI, Pope. *Encyclical Letter Deus Caritas Est.* December 25, 2005. https://www.vatican.va/content/benedict-xvi/en/encyclicals/documents/hf_ben-xvi_enc_20051225_deus-caritas-est.html.

Monographs

De Meester, Conrad. *The Power of Confidence: Genesis and Structure of the "Way of Spiritual Childhood" of Saint Thérèse of Lisieux.* Translated by Susan Conroy. New York: Alba House, 1998.

Descouvemont, P. *Thérèse of Lisieux and Marie of the Trinity: The Transformative Relationship of Saint Thérèse of Lisieux and Her Novice Sr. Marie of the Trinity.* New York: Alba House, 1997.

Descouvemont, P. *Thérèse de Lisieux et son prochain.* Paris: Les Éditions du Cerf, 2003.

Ermatinger, C. *St. Thérèse of Lisieux, Spouse and Victim.* Washington, D.C.: ICS Publications, 2010.

Gaucher, Guy. *Saint Thérèse of Lisieux: The Story of a Life.* San Francisco: Ignatius Press, 2019.

Gaucher, Guy. *Sainte Thérèse de Lisieux (1873–1897): Biographie.* Paris: Les Éditions du Cerf, 2010.

Gaucher, Guy. *The Passion of Thérèse of Lisieux: 4 April–30 September 1897.* New York: The Crossroad Publishing Company, 1990.

González, Luis Jorge. *Teresa di Lisieux: Intelligenza emotiva e Counseling spirituale.* Roma: Edizioni OCD, 2019.

Céline Martin and Sœur Cécile, eds. La Bible avec Thérèse de Lisieux. Paris: Les Éditions du Cerf, 1990.

Les mots de Sainte Thérèse de l'Enfant-Jésus et de la Sainte-Face: Concordance générale. Established by Soeur Geneviève, O.P., and Soeur Cécile, O.C.D. Lonrai: Les Éditions du Cerf, 1996.

Niyitegeka, Cyprien. *The Metaphor of the Face in Thérèse of Lisieux from the Philosophical Perspective of Emmanuel Lévinas: Creating a Model for Contemporary Mission Spirituality.* Washington, D.C.: The Catholic University of America, 2017.

Patrizi, M.E. *Il Patto segreto: L'amicizia mistica di san Massimiliano Kolbe e santa Teresa di Lisieux.* Roma: C.d.C. Editrice, 2008.

Descouvemont, P., H.N. Loose, and D. Leprince, eds. *Sainte Thérèse de Lisieux: La vie en images.* Paris: Cerf, 1995.

Spence, Joseph. *Un'esperienza sponsale con Dio: l'influsso di san Giovanni della Croce su santa Teresa di Lisieux.* Tesi di dottorato, Pontificia Facoltà Teologica "Teresianum," Roma, 2020.

Loose, H.M., P. Descouvemont, and D. Leprince. *Thérèse et Lisieux.* Paris: Cerf, 1991.

Articles

Assailly, A. "Thérèse, sœur des hommes dans les épreuves." *Annales de Sainte Thérèse de Lisieux* 2 (1973): 7–12.

"De nouveaux CSM [Conseils et Souvenirs de Marie de la Trinité] (no. 31–57)." *VT* 77 (1980).

Gayral, L. "Une maladie nerveuse dans l'enfance de Sainte Thérèse de Lisieux." *Carmel* (1959): 81–96.

Maître, J. *L'Orpheline de la Béresina: Thérèse de Lisieux (1873–1897).* Paris: Cerf, 1996, 194–202.

Patrizi, M.E. "'La mia vocazione è l'amore.' Sulla scia di Maria." *Rivista di Vita Spirituale* 6 (1997): 753–762.

Patrizi, M.E. "P. Kolbe e la spiritualità di Santa Teresa di Gesù Bambino." *Rivista di Vita Spirituale* 53 (1999): 188–209.

Patrizi, M.E. "S. Teresa di Lisieux: 'Nella Chiesa io sarò l'amore.'" *La Madonna delle Laste* 11 (1996): 11.

Spence, J. "Dio Padre nell'esperienza e nella teologia di santa Teresa di Lisieux: un segno di speranza per il mondo di oggi" ("God the Father in the Experience and the Theology of Saint Thérèse of Lisieux: A Sign of Hope for the World Today"). In *Ripensare la teologia con santa Teresa di Lisieux. Atti del Seminario di approfondimento (*Pontifica Facoltà Teologica Teresianum, Roma, 23-24 maggio 2024)*, Theologie der Spiritualität. Quellen und studien 14, EOS Verlag Sankt Ottilien, Germany 2025.

Spence J., « *Una memoria "vivente": la rilettura di san Giovanni della Croce da parte di santa Teresa di Lisieux*», Teresianum 70 (2019/2), 583–607.